D1262193

AN ILLUSTRATED TREASURY OF

Cultivated

BY FRANK J. ANDERSON

HONORARY CURATOR OF RARE BOOKS

NEW YORK BOTANICAL GARDEN

ABBEVILLE PRESS • PUBLISHERS • NEW YORK

Flowers

FRONT COVER
Periwinkle Varieties
Vinca minor varieties

Commentary on page 136

TITLE PAGE
Chinese Peony
Paeonia albiflora

Commentary on page 96

The illustrations in this book are from the collection of the New York Botanical Garden and are reproduced by permission of the Garden's president, Dr. Howard S. Irwin, and the director of the Library, Mr. Charles R. Long.

LC 79–64989

ISBN 0–89659–066–6

CONTENTS

Christmas Rose and Carnation 12–13
HELLEBORUS NIGER and DIANTHUS CARYOPHYLLUS

Pansy Varieties 14–15
VIOLA TRICOLOR varieties

Campion 16–17
LYCHNIS GRANDIFLORA

Blue Gentian 18–19
GENTIANA ACAULIS

Cinquefoil 20–21
POTENTILLA ATROSANGUINEA

Magnolia 22–23
MAGNOLIA ACUMINATA

Yellow Lady-slipper 24–25
CYPRIPEDIUM CALCEOLUS

Corn Poppy 26–27
PAPAVER RHOEAS

English Iris 28–29
IRIS XIPHIOIDES

Tigerflower 30–31
TIGRIDIA PAVONIA variety CONCHIFLORA

Columbine 32–33
AQUILEGIA VULGARIS

Blue Columbine 34–35
AQUILEGIA VULGARIS variety

King Frederick Tulip 36–37
TULIPA variety FREDERICUS REX

Sweet Pea 38–39
LATHYRUS ODORATUS

Tree Peony 40–41
PAEONIA SUFFRUTICOSA

Bluebell-of-Scotland 42–43
CAMPANULA ROTUNDIFOLIA

Gesner's Tulip 44–45
TULIPA GESNERIANA

Bleeding Heart 46–47
DICENTRA SPECTABILIS

Snowball Tree 48–49
VIBURNUM TOMENTOSUM variety PLICATUM

Cabbage Rose 50–51
ROSA CENTIFOLIA

Dayflower 52–53
COMMELINA COELESTIS

Turk's Cap Lily 54–55
LILIUM SUPERBUM

Evening Primrose 56–57
OENOTHERA BIENNIS

Japanese Iris 58–59
IRIS KAEMPFERI

Virginia Cowslip 60–61
MERTENSIA VIRGINICA

Everlasting Pea 62–63
LATHYRUS LATIFOLIUS

Blue Geranium 64–65
GERANIUM PRATENSE

Lilac 66–67
SYRINGA VULGARIS

Zinnia 68–69
ZINNIA ELEGANS

Spanish Iris 70–71
IRIS XIPHIUM

Bee-balm or Oswego Tea 72–73
MONARDA DIDYMA

Narcissus 74–75
NARCISSUS TAZETTA

Blue or Great Lobelia 76–77
LOBELIA SIPHILITICA

Yellow Rose and Rose of India 78–79
ROSA LUTEA and ROSA INDICA

Monkshood 80–81
ACONITUM NAPELLUS

Wallflower 82–83
CHEIRANTHUS CHEIRI variety

Forget-me-not 84–85
MYOSOTIS SCORPIOIDES

Carnation 86–87
DIANTHUS CARYOPHYLLUS

China Aster 88–89
CALLISTEPHUS CHINENSIS

Tickseed 90–91
COREOPSIS TINCTORIA

Lord Chatham's Tulip 92–93
TULIPA variety LORD CHATHAM

Downy Thorn Apple 94–95
DATURA FASTUOSA

Chinese Peony 96–97
PAEONIA ALBIFLORA

Fringed Iris 98–99
IRIS JAPONICA

Peony 100–101
PAEONIA OFFICINALIS

Blue Windflower 102–103
ANEMONE BLANDA variety ATROCAERULEA

Peruvian Lily 104–105
ALSTROMERIA AURANTIACA

Fritillary 106–107
FRITILLARIA MELEAGRIS

Red-hot Poker 108–109
KNIPHOFIA UVARIA

Auricula 110–111
PRIMULA AURICULA

Honesty 112–113
LUNARIA ANNUA

French Marigold 114–115
TAGETES PATULA

Balm 116–117
MELITTIS MELISSOPHYLLUM

Crown Imperial 118–119
FRITILLARIA IMPERIALIS

Meadow Sage 120–121
SALVIA PRATENSIS

Butterfly Weed 122–123
ASCLEPIAS TUBEROSA

Foxglove 124–125
DIGITALIS PURPUREA

Pansy 126–127
VIOLA TRICOLOR

Pelargonium Hybrids 128–129
PELARGONIUM DAVEYANUM varieties

Hollyhock 130–131
ALCEA ROSEA

Dutch Iris 132–133
IRIS XIPHIUM variety

Amaryllis 134–135
AMARYLLIS BELLADONNA

Periwinkle Varieties 136–137
VINCA MINOR varieties

Hyacinth 138–139
HYACINTHUS ORIENTALIS

Windflower 140–141
ANEMONE CORONARIA

Snapdragon 142–143
ANTIRRHINUM MAJUS

Sunflower 144–145
HELIANTHUS ANNUUS

Stonecrop 146–147
ROCHEA COCCINEA

Plantain Lily 148–149
HOSTA SIEBOLDIANA

Canterbury Bells 150–151
CAMPANULA MEDIUM

Cornflower 152–153
CENTAUREA CYANUS

Japanese Anemone 154–155
ANEMONE JAPONICA

Avens 156–157
GEUM CHILOENSE

INTRODUCTION

CULTIVATION AND CIVILIZATION go hand in hand, for it was not until man learned how to direct the bounty he found in the natural world about him that he began to rise to a civilized condition. So long as his full attention was devoted to hunting and gathering, there was neither leisure nor opportunity to develop the means of making life a pleasanter and more rewarding experience. Birds and lilies may "sow not, neither do they reap" nor "toil not, neither do they spin," but they still pay a price for their apparent ease. This cost is *total* dependence on outside forces, without the slightest chance of influencing them in return.

Once man learned how to raise food instead of hunting for it, his progress became astonishing. Within the past 10,000 years he has advanced farther than in the previous 1,990,000; from being a hunter who was often hunted himself, he has become capable of altering climate, probing the processes of life itself, and even moving beyond the boundaries of Earth. And all of those privileges and possibilities have grown out of the simple fact that agriculture bought the necessary time to pursue other goals than chasing after food.

With the first communities there also came the beginnings of government, architecture, trade, and settled conditions that made life a little less hazardous and frightening than it had been. At last there was time to create beautiful and pleasurable things, among them the arts; one of these, a natural outgrowth of agriculture, was gardening—the art of cultivating flowers.

Despite the fact that horticulture is necessarily among the most inexact of sciences, being rooted in all the infinite variabilities of the life processes, genetics, and climate, it is far from being an impractical pursuit. One indispensable function it performs is to nourish the human psyche, a process no less valuable, for being unmeasurable, than is the physical development of a child. In more visible areas, the techniques and developments of horticulture have greatly affected not only the appearance of the world we live in, but the quality of the food we eat, the supply of paper for our endless communication, and everything else that is furnished by the plant world, from perfume to hormones.

A continuing interest in plants, and a concern for their welfare and survival, is among the most practical and realistic of basic activities. Without plants we would soon cease to exist, for they are not only the base of the food chain upon which all life depends, but they also replenish the earth's supply of oxygen. There is far more hardheaded practicality involved in learning how to keep plants alive and well than in constructing the most profound analysis of the stock market. After all, what stock can return a thousand for one, and continually renew its physical assets from little more than sunlight, air, water, and a microscopic amount of chemicals?

History is filled with instances of both the powerful and the intelligent becoming captivated by the appeal of plants. Queen Hatshepsut organized the first expedition to import useful plants from foreign sources in the fifteenth century B.C., and Alexander the Great, in the fourth century B.C., took time from his conquests to send plants from as far off as India back to Athens for study. In the first century A.D. both Dioscorides, a Greek physician, and Pliny, the Roman administrator and historian, wrote copious works on plants, medicinal and otherwise, while in the eighteenth century Carl Linné, with a mind as precise and analytical as a modern computer, created a system of classification that distinguished any plant from all others, using only two descriptive terms for each plant.

Gardens and gardening have been part of every major civilization from Egypt down to the present. The great villas beside the Nile were built within walls that protected the plantings from the fierce heat of desert winds; the ancient Egyptians grew sycamore figs, grape vines, pomegranates, and tamarisks beside pools lined with cornflowers, poppies, and lotus blossoms. In Rome life was made more delightful by shady arbors, olive and cypress trees, and roses growing by the thousands. The Arab empire, from Persia and Baghdad to the gardens of the Alhambra, was filled with the scents of jasmine, roses, myrtle, and the sound of water splashing in courtyard fountains or rippling quietly in channels and plant-rimmed pools. Italy and France created formally patterned gardens that imposed design and discipline upon wayward nature, while the English, with a confidence born of power, subjected the entire landscape to manmade rules so as to recast nature into an ideal image unmarred by any imperfection.

Gardens have contributed mightily to the concept of art in every age and have created decorative styles as divergent as those of China, where the infinite and the intimate were made to dwell together, are from those of the Aztecs, where jungle, mountains, plains, and desert were all brought into harmony and arranged for study as well as display. Artists have always found inspiration in the shapes and colors of flowers, and it is difficult to envision the organic design of any flower or tree being excelled in inventiveness and interest by any school of painters or designers. The logic of nature's patterns is the basic alphabet, which cannot be surpassed, but only utilized and restated in endless permutations.

Oddly enough, the beauty of plants has not always been as self-evident as it seems to us today. Men were more interested in what could be done with plants than in how they looked. Medicinal, nutritional, practical, and commercial uses were once uppermost considerations, and we have literally had to learn to see these miracles and marvels of beauty that have always been before our eyes. Prehistoric man took more pains to render the outlines of animals, his main article of diet, than he ever did with the depiction of such unimportant things as plants. Later there were religions that preached against the snares and delusions with which nature and its arsenal of devilish temptations continually surrounded us. Still farther down the line, plants were relegated to a subordinate position in the arts, as opposed to human and animal forms, and were only considered fit for design patterns, symbols, or emblems until as recently as post-Renaissance times.

Not until the great age of exploration in the sixteenth century, with the consequent discovery and introduction of hundreds and thousands of new species, did the arts of flower painting and gardening truly begin to flourish. With the concurrent development of printing, images could at last be multiplied easily and distributed to every civilized corner of the globe. Herbals such as Gerard's, with their pictures of medicinal plants, and horticultural works such as Parkinson's *Earthly Paradise,* with their profusion of woodcuts, created an ever greater demand for plant images even in the very act of satisfying it. Soon techniques of etching, engraving, and lithography were devised that improved the quality and capabilities of the graphic arts in depicting plants. Today we have photography and photoengraving, processes which can reproduce aspects of the plant world that would otherwise be impossible to capture; but for truly outstanding craftsmanship, artistic sensitivity, and fidelity to detail, the master engravers and lithographers of the eighteenth and nineteenth centuries have never been surpassed. In the following pages you will sample the work of such artists as Georg Ehret, who introduced much of Europe to the wealth of beauty with which America was supplying its gardens. And there is Pierre-Joseph Redouté, whose eye and hand not only equaled the clarity and precision of the photoengraving process, but at times excelled it. There are also the great, and often anonymous, lithographers of the Victorian era's horticultural journals, which did more to popularize gardening and spread its gospel than had been done in all the ages before.

Any garden is a world in miniature, with living plants that may have originated in every corner of the earth. It is also a controlled environment where we can create our own "paradise," a Persian word that means nothing more than "park." And who does not think of his or her garden as a parkland where dimensions and pleasures are measured not by the yardstick but by the soul?

Gardens, of course, need care, so each garden plant shown here is accompanied by directions as to how it should be planted and raised. These, however, should not be considered rigid dogmas, but more in the nature of guidelines, for every garden in the world has its own world within itself, and each of these worlds has its own set of rules. The plants themselves will teach you more than volumes of instructions, and should be heeded before all else.

Simply remember that gardening is an art, and that the practice of any art leads to expertise in it.

Whether you find shrubs, bulbs, annuals, or perennials the most absorbing elements of your garden, samples of all of them have been provided for your delight by the great botanical artists of the past. Their histories, origins, and the secrets and poetry of their names are set forth as well, together with some of their forgotten or unexpected uses. Some of the hidden workings of plant life are brought into view, and throughout the book each plant is given its own character, made into something more than a silent, green thing that just sits there and grows. The cultivation of flowers has but one main end: to open the way to a richer, deeper life, filled with a better understanding of the many forms of life that share this earth with us.

AN ILLUSTRATED TREASURY OF

Cultivated Flowers

Christmas Rose and Carnation

[HELLEBORUS NIGER and DIANTHUS CARYOPHYLLUS]

THE ROOTS OF THE CHRISTMAS ROSE, which are violently purgative and poisonous, were used from antiquity down to the seventeenth century as a cure for insanity. No doubt most of the patients who received the plant were relieved of their eccentricities and violence on a permanent basis, but such "treatment" could hardly be called a cure. A pleasanter legend about the plant tells of a young girl who found that she had no gift for Christ on the night of His birth, and wept until an angel caused her tears to turn into blossoms, which the child then happily gathered as a present.

As far as the historical accuracy of its name is concerned, the Christmas rose does blossom in late fall, and also in December or even late winter; but, unluckily for the tale, the flower is native to Europe but not to the Holy Land. It is a most persistent plant, and some specimens have been known to bloom unattended for more than fifty years around abandoned cottages. Generally they were planted there to keep evil from the house, since the flower was associated with Christ's nativity. The carnation is also shown here as a symbol of Christ's embodiment at Christmastide.

Helleborus niger prefers a moist, well-drained soil, somewhat porous, with humus and a bit of lime worked into it. It needs sun in winter, but shade in summer. In regions that drop below zero for any appreciable time it may die off, even with protection. It is sensitive to being uprooted, so avoid transplanting; it may take two to three years to bloom again after being moved. Depending on the locality, it may bloom at any time from November through March, when its six- to twelve-inch stems will provide a welcome profusion of cut flowers.

Carnations may be treated as hardy perennials in regions with mild winters, such as California or the coastal areas of the Carolinas and Georgia. Where the temperature drops to zero or a bit below, only the *very* hardy varieties, developed in recent years, should be planted, and they must have winter protection. Any good, light soil in a well-drained location will do. Sow seed in flats in very early spring, and move seedlings outdoors after frost has ended. Or set out plants in late spring, either purchased or made from cuttings, placing them 10 inches apart. Some of the newer border carnations are perpetual-flowering, and provide fragrant cut flowers throughout the summer.

Pansy Varieties

[VIOLA TRICOLOR Varieties]

INTENSIVE AND SKILLED BREEDING of pansies, responsible for the many kinds now available to gardeners, did not get under way until the nineteenth century. The major figure in its early stages was Lord Gambier's gardener, Thompson, who developed so many kinds that he had to ransack the pages of Shakespeare to find names for all of them. By 1841, some twenty-nine years after the modest beginnings of its cultivation, over four hundred named varieties were known. English, French, and Belgian strains were crossed to create the ancestors of the flowers we know today, gradually improving hardiness, color, and form. The garden varieties shown here are distinguished by their large size and solid colors, in contrast to the smaller, three-hued flowers of *Viola tricolor*.

Pansies do best in a rich garden soil, placed where they can be kept in cool shade and where their roots will not dry out. Plantings should be rotated every two or three years to avoid root disease. Although it may grow as a biennial or perennial, the plant is best treated as an annual, since it has a tendency to straggle and to produce smaller, weaker flowers if carried over. Sow seeds thinly in spring, in shallow rows about ⅛ inch deep. Use powdery soil that has been mixed with rotted manure and thoroughly watered, and keep it gently sprayed and shaded while seeds are sprouting. Thin out areas that grow too quickly, and pluck flowers before they set seed to lengthen the period of bloom.

Campion

[LYCHNIS GRANDIFLORA]

CAMPIONS HAVE BEEN CULTIVATED for centuries, and their brilliant scarlet or crimson flowers always make an eye-catching display. The scientific name *Lychnis* comes from the Greek for lamp, referring to the flame-colored flowers of species such as this one. Its common names, campion and catchfly, refer to its habit of growing in fields (*campi* in Latin) and to the plant's sticky stems, which trap small insects that blunder up against them. It is a member of the pink family, as may be guessed from the jagged edges of its petals, which look as if they were trimmed by pinking shears.

Campion is a biennial with flowers two inches in diameter. It originated in the Far East; whether the exact locale was Japan or China remains unknown. It grows to a height of eighteen inches in any moderately rich and well-drained garden soil, blooming from late June until frost. Since it is half-hardy, the seed should be started indoors in flats during March and moved out in April after frost, placed where it will receive either full sun or some light shade. The soil should be well turned to a spade's depth before planting. These flowers are well adapted to the north temperate zone, and make excellent plants for the border or for the cutting garden. The roots of this species may be divided for propagation.

Blue Gentian

[G E N T I A N A   A C A U L I S]

GENTIANA ACAULIS, which means stemless gentian, has long been a favorite garden flower, in spite of the difficulties it creates for the gardener. It was among the first plants chosen for the gardens of the eighteenth-century Blenheim Palace, being prized for its bright, blazing blue blossoms. In earlier times gentians were noted for their medicinal properties, and figure in ancient Egyptian, Greek, and Roman prescriptions. The genus is named for Gentius, King of Illyria, who is said to have discovered its medical virtues and to have relied upon it as an antidote to poison. It does have antiseptic value, and is effective in killing intestinal worms and controlling fever; it is also recognized as a tonic whose bitter glucosides are an aid in treating dyspepsia and jaundice. One of its medieval names, felwort, meaning bitter plant, refers directly to its harsh flavor.

G. acaulis is an Alpine perennial that blooms in May, displaying a densely packed cushion of deep strong blue, though in some years the blossoms end almost as fast as they begin. It demands a rich, deep soil, since the roots plunge well into the earth. An ample supply of moisture is also needed, but it must drain off readily. In its natural location the broken rocks of alpine scree perform that service for it, but in the garden a generous layer of crushed limestone will make a perfectly good substitute, for *G. acaulis* is a plant that loves lime. In skilled hands it is well worth growing, but otherwise it should be left alone.

Cinquefoil

[POTENTILLA ATROSANGUINEA]

A RELATIVE OF THE ROSE, this genus has long been associated with man through medicine, magic, and ornamental gardening. This species, *Potentilla atrosanguinea,* stands for "powerful and dark red," in reference to its splashes of color. It comes from the Himalayas, and entered cultivation very early in the nineteenth century; its great popularity in the garden was even further enhanced by the improvements developed in it through hybridization.

In Tibet its roots, tiny and nutlike, are used as a food, and reportedly taste like asparagus or new potatoes. Occidental species have also been used as foodstuff, and *Potentilla* once formed part of a fish lure, spread on fishing nets to insure a good catch. The genus is rich in tannin and has strong astringent properties; its leaves are used to brew tea, treat fevers, tan leather, and as a styptic preparation, while its flowers are used in dyeing. The plant has also been used in witchcraft, in an ointment that included flour, monkshood, wild celery, and the fat of a dead child. It was said that "the toad will be much under sage, frogs will be in cinquefoil."

Potentilla atrosanguinea is herbaceous and perennial, persisting for many years wherever it is planted. It blooms from June to August in the open border in any good garden soil. Start seeds in sandy soil in early spring, planted ⅛ inch deep in seed flats that have been placed in a cold frame. Plant outdoors as soon as seedlings are large enough to be handled. Every third year divide the rootstock. Seed for the species shown here may now be rare, but similar hybrids are available.

Magnolia

[MAGNOLIA ACUMINATA]

WHILE MANY MAGNOLIAS start off as mere shrubs, a number of them develop into stately trees. *Magnolia acuminata,* a deciduous species sometimes known as cucumber tree, can reach a height of one hundred feet. It is native to the eastern United States, where it can be found in coastal areas as far north as southern Massachusetts. Its wood is soft, light, and durable, but lacks the strength needed for heavy usage.

Magnolias, along with buttercups, are the most primitive of flowering plants, and have an ancestral record that predates man by more than sixty million years. About eighty species are known, some deciduous, some evergreen, of all sizes from shrubs to very tall trees. The genus was named for Pierre Magnol, a seventeenth-century physician and botanist who lived in Montpellier, France.

The magnolia flowers anytime between mid-May and mid-June, depending on the latitude. A good, deep hole should be prepared for the tree in springtime, and the roots kept covered until actual planting so they won't dry out. Great care should be taken so as to avoid any damage to the root system. Their chief requirement after planting is a site with good drainage. Well-rotted manure may be placed around the base of the tree once every two or three years. Do not prune, except to remove dead or damaged branches, and avoid transplanting if at all possible. Should that become necessary, however, never do it in the fall.

Yellow Lady-slipper

[CYPRIPEDIUM CALCEOLUS]

ONCE UPON A TIME LADY-SLIPPER was rarely grown in gardens, although John Gerard, the Elizabethan herbalist, grew it in his, as did John Tradescant of Lambeth a little later on. Since it was a wild plant found in bogs and wet woodlands, it was obviously not the easiest thing to raise in ordinary soil. Physicians, however, had found a use for it as a tranquilizer and a sedative, so efforts to raise it persisted. Its medicinal uses are reflected in its English and German names, nerve-root and *Nervenwurzel*. Among its other names are Virgin Mary's shoe, parson's shoe, yellow shoe, cuckoo's shoe, and Venus slipper.

Cypripedium calceolus is hardy as far north as southern Canada. Rhizomes of the plant are now available from nurseries and are much easier to raise than any gathered from the wild, where, in any case, they are becoming rather rare. Start them as soon as frost is over by placing them in moist, well-drained soil enriched with humus. Cover the crown of the rhizome with about an inch of soil, being careful not to pack it down tightly. Do not water until shoots appear, and then gradually increase the supply as the shoots and buds develop, giving most at the time of bloom in May and June. Gradually decrease the supply after bloom is over, and give no water to the dormant plant. Provide partial shade in spring and summer.

Corn Poppy

[PAPAVER RHOEAS]

THIS IS THE FAMILIAR red poppy of World War I days, the one that blossomed in Flanders' fields "between the crosses, row on row." It is also the ancestor of the Shirley poppy, which was bred in the English town of that name and not, as some might suppose, named after a person. For centuries this flower has dotted the grain fields of Europe, springing up unbidden amidst the stalks of wheat. By no means as potent as the opium poppy, *Papaver rhoeas* still possesses some narcotic properties, and has been used as a milder substitute. The seeds, mixed with honey, were formerly used as a remedy for intestinal troubles, while the leaves and heads used to be applied to the skin to reduce inflammation. An unstable dye extracted from the flowers is still used to color wines and medicines.

Papaver, of course, is simply the Latin word for poppy, and *rhoeas* means wild poppy. These somewhat redundant terms reinforce our notion of this species as the quintessential poppy.

Sow poppy seed in autumn in light, loamy soil enriched with humus. In regions of exceptional cold, plant in springtime. Place them in a spot where there is ample sun and leave sufficient room for the plants to develop properly. *P. rhoeas* is an annual that may be reseeded each fall, though it often does so on its own.

English Iris

[IRIS XIPHIOIDES]

ALTHOUGH IT IS CALLED English iris, *Iris xiphioides* actually comes from the Pyrenees. It is also native to the same region as *I. xiphium*, the Spanish iris, of which it may well be a subspecies. It acquired the name English iris because it was found growing wild in the fields of western England, around such places as the port of Bristol. Sixteenth-century botanists thought it to be a native plant when in fact it had simply escaped into the wild from gardens, where it had been planted by travelers returning to Bristol from Spain. Bristol imported and distributed vast quantities of Spanish sherry—so much so that the wine came to be called Bristol milk and Bristol cream throughout much of England. Undoubtedly some of the British merchants had admired *I. xiphioides* in its own land and brought home samples for planting.

Like *I. xiphium*, the English flower is a bulbous iris, without rhizomes. This physical trait led to some of its early botanical names at a time when botanists, herbalists, and gardeners were struggling to find practical labels for the staggering amount of plant life they found around them. John Gerard called it *Iris bulbosa anglica*, the onion floure-de-luce, while John Parkinson lengthened the name slightly to *Iris bulbosa maior sive anglica caerulea,* the "great blue English flower-de-luce." It blooms from May to August in damp, sandy places.

English iris likes a medium soil, not too rich, and without lime, contrary to early practice. Place the bulbs (this species has no rhizomes) where they will receive plenty of sun and good drainage, for it is necessary to keep the soil moist but never wet and soggy. The bulbs should be set about 6 inches apart and covered with 3 to 4 inches of soil that has been well spaded and forked so as to keep it open and aerated. About 8 to 10 inches below the bulbs, a layer of compost may be placed to aid drainage and to give nourishment. Some low-nitrogen fertilizer or rotted manure may be mixed in, but it should not be allowed to come into contact with the bulbs. A light layer of earth, spread over the compost and fertilizer, will prevent that from happening. Water the bulbs frequently after planting, but less so as they approach blooming. In winter protect plants with a mulch.

Tigerflower

[TIGRIDIA PAVONIA Variety CONCHIFLORA]

IT IS KNOWN THAT *Tigridia pavonia* was indeed named for the eighteenth-century Spanish explorer José Pavon. Had that not been so, then the translation from the botanical Latin would have been the "tiger-peacock." Add to that the variety's terms *conchi,* mollusk, plus *flora,* flower, and you have a magnificently impossible composite—a striped tiger with a peacock's tail, oozing about the garden on a snaillike foot, while wearing a garland of flowers beneath a shell-like helmet! It makes a subject fit for Hieronymus Bosch, or else it could be a psychic phantasm rising to trouble the air above a psychiatrist's couch.

In Mexico, the tigerflower's native habitat, the bulbs are often baked as an article of food, yet in Europe (where it was not grown) it took almost three hundred years just for people to come to believe in its existence. Why they balked at accepting this flower when they had already granted full approval to the fictitious vegetable lamb of Tartary is a question that remains unanswerable.

Tigridias may be planted outdoors just before summer, placed 3 inches deep in soil that is a mixture of loam, sand, and humus. It is important that the area be well drained; a layer of broken pots or cut stone may be added at a depth of about 18 inches to ensure proper runoff. Be certain that the plants get plenty of sun, but make provision to shelter them from any cold drafts that might develop. Keep the soil moist in dry weather by watering and mulching. When the plants' foliage dies down in fall, lift and dry the bulbs and put them in a dry, cool, but coldproof place for winter storage. Replant next season.

Columbine

[AQUILEGIA VULGARIS]

NO TWO PEOPLE EVER SEE ANYTHING in exactly the same way, a fact of which this plant is living proof. One man saw in it a resemblance to the eagle standard of the Roman legions and used the Latin word for eagle, *aquila,* in naming the plant. Another gardener likened the flower to a group of doves touching beak to beak and called it *columba,* Latin for dove. The resemblance to the dove also led to columbine's becoming a Christian symbol of the Holy Spirit, who was often depicted as a white dove descending.

This species, probably the best known of all columbines, originated in the Eurasian region well before the beginning of recorded history. It blooms in the summer, when its nodding flowers, about two inches wide and borne on stalks two to four feet high, make a good display in any open border. Generally blue, the blossoms may sometimes be white or lilac instead.

Aquilegia vulgaris does best in an open, sunny situation in soil of sandy loam; the perennial border is a natural spot for it. Columbines can be propagated easily by dividing their clumps in the springtime. Excessively rainy summers may discourage or even kill the plant; but with its sturdy genetic heritage, most columbines will thrive in a temperate climate.

Blue Columbine

[AQUILEGIA VULGARIS Variety]

THE COLUMBINE HAS BEEN familiar as both a medicinal and a garden plant through all of western Asia and Europe since ancient times. It was formerly prescribed for liver obstructions and stones in the kidney and bladder, and was mixed with wine and ambergris in a concoction believed to reduce the tendency to faint. What was unknown in earlier ages, although it had begun to be suspected, was that columbine had poisonous properties. In the mid-eighteenth century Linnaeus, who was a physician as well as a taxonomist, advised against its use, particularly with children, citing cases of poisoning from large doses. Columbine is related rather closely to the beautiful but frequently dangerous buttercup family, which includes the very deadly aconites.

Aquilegia vulgaris was once known in early Britain as the culverwort, a Saxon term for "dove plant." It is identical in meaning to columbine, which comes from the Latin for dove, *columba*. The plant was also known as boots and shoes, cock's foot, dove's foot, granny's nightcap, hawk's feet, lady's shoes, and two-faces-under-a-hat.

The giant spurs on many of the new varieties, some of which exhibit contrasting colors on the same flower, result from hybridizing columbines from the Rocky Mountains and California, *A. coerulea* and *A. chrysantha* respectively. They are spectacular plants, but if you want to keep them breeding true don't put any other columbines in their neighborhood, or you will get unwanted hybrids.

For culture see Columbine (page 32).

King Frederick Tulip

[T U L I P A Variety F R E D E R I C U S R E X]

THE PHENOMENON OF THE "broken" or striped tulip was observed almost from the time that tulips became garden flowers in Europe. Such tulips were regarded as rarities and were highly prized, particularly when the markings were vivid and evenly distributed inward from the edges of the petals. One such tulip, called *Semper Augustus,* was first offered for sale in 1623 at a price of about $1800, and still sold some thirteen years later for an almost identical amount. Only twelve bulbs of the variety were known in 1624, and scarcely any increase in the supply occurred in the next decade.

Striped tulips cannot be bred from seed, for they result from a virus that does not affect the chromosomes. They can be bred only from offsets of the parent bulbs, and quite often the prized pattern will not recur spontaneously for many years. High cost and unreliability eventually led to their disappearance. The King Frederick tulip of the eighteenth century is only history now, but is shown here as an example of the standards of beauty held in the past and as a sample of Georg Ehret's excellent botanical art.

When any group of tulips is planted year after year, especially in warm, light soil lacking in richness, the virus that forms these spectacular breaks may occur. The class of tulips known as breeders is probably best for those who want to try to raise tulips with this broken pattern. Two types of markings are found on pure white grounds: "feathered," which is largely confined to the edges, and "flamed," which covers a much larger area of the petals.

Tulip bulbs should be planted late in the fall, about the middle of October, in a bed previously well spaded, and with commercial fertilizer worked into the soil. Holes about 6 inches deep should be made with a dibble, and an inch of gritty sand put into them. Set the bulb on top of the sand and cover it with earth. After blooming, let the plants remain until the leaves have withered. By then the bulbs should have stored enough food for the next season and can be lifted for drying and storage in a cool, dry place until replanting time. Very often, however, tulips are treated as annuals and discarded after their display is over.

Sweet Pea

[LATHYRUS ODORATUS]

THIS LONGTIME GARDEN FAVORITE first began its career as a wild flower in Sicily, and came into cultivation there during the 1600s. Only a handful of varieties were available in its early days, and it made little horticultural impact until the 1870s, when one Henry Eckford greatly improved the colors and shape of the sweet pea, even increasing the number of blooms that it bore. During the first decade of this century it became an almost ubiquitous element in table decorations, where its delicate colors and fragrance had rapidly made it a prime favorite. For that matter, it still retains much of its old popularity even today, for it exemplifies just about everything we enjoy and admire in flowers.

Unlike the everlasting pea, the sweet pea is an annual plant. It does not take kindly to hot weather; if the thermometer remains above 75° F. for any appreciable time it will soon fade away. Luckily, it can be grown in a cool greenhouse, at about 50° F., and will then flower from winter right through early spring. Wherever outdoor summer temperatures are generally too high for this species, it should be sown in a cold frame early in October and given good ventilation until frost, when the frames should be well covered. Uncover in very early spring and transplant the seedlings after frost, placing them about 5 inches apart. They will thus be well established by the time hot summer arrives, and may make it through July if some shading is given. Their plot should be spaded twice, with well-rotted manure and some good commercial fertilizer worked in. Plenty of moisture and additional nourishment should be given while it is growing. In the greenhouse, 10-inch pots filled with a rich soil and watered frequently should accomplish the same result. Start plants in 3-inch pots in August (for winter) or November (for spring), and move them to the larger pots before the roots become potbound. Whether grown indoors or outdoors, sweet pea always needs support, from either chicken wire or thin stakes planted on either side.

Tree Peony

[PAEONIA SUFFRUTICOSA]

THE COMMON NAME FOR THIS lovely plant is really a slight exaggeration, since it is a shrub that rises only to about six feet at most. It is called tree peony because of the fact that it has rather woody stems, as its botanical name proclaims: *suffruticosa* means "somewhat woody" or "half-shrub." Other peonies have herbaceous stems, similar to those of flowers but heavier in structure.

P. suffruticosa originated in China, where it came to be known as the King of Flowers. But centuries of breeding had to be expended on the wild plant before it could produce the shrub that we see today. As a reward to all those anonymous Chinese gardeners who developed it, the plant is now sold as the Japanese tree peony, because the growers in Japan were the first to commercialize it in the West.

Cultivational directions for this peony may be found under *Paeonia officinalis* (page 100), but *disregard* the instruction there to cut the growth back to the ground in the fall. This peony has permanent woody growth above ground, and if that is cut back there won't be any plant. When placing a tree peony in the ground provide a deep hole for it, one sufficient to bury the scion, that portion of the plant which is grafted onto the root stock, halfway into the ground. Partial shade will benefit the blossoms.

Bluebell-of-Scotland

[CAMPANULA ROTUNDIFOLIA]

CAMPANULAS HAVE ALWAYS BEEN favorite garden flowers, and have had other uses as well. One species, throatwort, was used as a gargle; it also bore the interesting name of bats-in-the-belfry. Another species called rampion was formerly grown for salads and its edible roots. Its botanical name, *Campanula rapunculus,* entered into one of Grimm's fairy tales. A villager had stolen this plant for his pregnant wife and was caught by the witch in whose garden it was growing. He was then obliged to promise the infant girl to the witch, and to name the child Rapunzel after the stolen plant. Yet another bluebell was grown in pots as a summertime decoration for empty fireplaces, and so became known as chimney bellflower. Still other species have gained the names of Venus's looking-glass and Canterbury bells.

Campanula rotundifolia is sometimes known as harebell, but more often as bluebell-of-Scotland. It is native to England and Scotland, but can easily be grown almost anywhere in the north temperate zone. It may be placed in the open border in almost any ordinary garden soil, and will bloom there in May or June. The plant may be started from seed sown after frost, but a safer and more certain method is to start the seeds indoors in February in shallow boxes of soil and move them to the border after all frost is over. As the plants increase within their area they may be divided in the spring and fall. They will tolerate some lime in the soil, but it is best not to add any.

Gesner's Tulip

[TULIPA GESNERIANA]

ANOTHER GIFT FROM THE SKILLED GARDENERS of sixteenth-century Turkey is the tulip, and this one is probably the first kind ever to bloom in Europe. Very possibly the tulip was known to the Persians even before the Turks took over its culture. In any case Babur, founder of the Mogul dynasty and himself a Turk, had tulips planted in his many gardens throughout Persia, Afghanistan, and India, and noted that they had been cultivated in his realm well before A.D. 1505, when he came to the throne. The name tulip comes from a misunderstanding of the Turkish word for turban, *dulban*, used as a simile in describing the plant to a European. In Turkish the tulip is never called anything but lâle.

The Gesner tulip honors the Swiss botanist Conrad Gesner, who discovered it in 1559, in an Augsburg garden. It is probably the ancestor of all common tulips growing today. Less than a century later, speculation in tulip bulbs had become so wild that in England, any single bulb was limited by law to a maximum price of £400.

For cultivation see *King Frederick Tulip* (page 36).

Bleeding Heart

[DICENTRA SPECTABILIS]

THE VARIETY OF NAMES that become attached to flowers is always amazing; in its way, it may be a form of folk poetry. In addition to the self-explanatory name of bleeding heart, there are a few more for the showy *Dicentra:* lyre flower and lady's locket, both reasonable; Chinaman's breeches, less so; and Our Lady in a boat, which gets well out of bounds. *Dicentra spectabilis* comes from China and, having been lost after its first trip to Europe, had to make the journey twice. Ever since its second introduction in 1846, it has been popular in gardens, but it can make trouble: all parts of the plant may cause dermatitis in persons sensitive to its irritant properties.

Although there are American species of the *Dicentra* genus, they need shade and rich woodland soil, so it is best to plant *Dicentra spectabilis* instead. It may be grown quite readily in the ordinary soil of any garden border, where its major requirement is partial shade. It blooms from spring through the summer, but dies back early in autumn, leaving a blank spot until the following season, unless one has had the foresight to place an autumn-blooming plant next to it. Modern varieties have given the plant improved color, profusion of bloom, and even two flowering seasons, early May to July and again in September. Some of the new varieties no longer require shade.

Snowball Tree

[VIBURNUM TOMENTOSUM Variety PLICATUM]

THE SOMEWHAT LENGTHY BOTANICAL NAME FOR THIS shrub simply means "the wayfaring tree with hairy, furrowed leaves." The "hairs" are the fuzz on the underside of the leaves, and the furrows are the deep venation on the upper surface. The shrub was found in China by the plant hunter Robert Fortune, who, though he couldn't speak the language, posed as a China-man so as to travel where foreigners were forbidden to go. He faked a barbarous dialect from a remote province, and used an interpreter to get by. When Fortune returned to London in 1846, *V. tomentosum* var. *plicatum* came back with him, along with dozens of other choice horticultural specimens, including the first forsythia to reach the West.

This variety of viburnum may reach seven to ten feet when fully grown, and is hardy in all but those places that experience long, severe winters. It is among the easiest of shrubs to cultivate, and will thrive in any ordinary garden soil with no more care than is given to a privet hedge. An open sunny spot is ideal for it. In May and June the plant displays its compact, rounded mass of flowers. By fall these produce numbers of small red fruits, which become a favorite food of birds as they ripen into a bluish-black. The leaves themselves take on vivid autumn hues. Since Fortune first returned with it, the shrub has remained a steady favorite.

Cabbage Rose

[ROSA CENTIFOLIA]

THE NUMEROUS PETALS of this flower gave rise to its Latin name, which means hundred-leaved rose. Its other common name, cabbage rose, comes from the fact that its blossoms are as full, firm, and densely packed as the heads of that garden vegetable. A distillation of its petals was once used in internal medicine; today the petals are used in making the lotion known as rose water or in the manufacture of scented preparations such as cold cream or potpourri. The major centers of such production are southern France, Morocco, and Bulgaria.

The rose was once the symbol of secrecy; when suspended above a conference or dining table, it was to be taken as a sign that nothing said beneath it should be repeated elsewhere, hence the Latin phrase *sub rosa*. At Roman banquets the flower symbolized pleasure, and its scent was thought to help prevent drunkenness.

Rosa centifolia originated in the Caucasus Mountains and is hardy in all but the coldest regions. It blooms once a year, usually in June, when it becomes laden with fragrant and extremely full blossoms. When planting the shrubs dig an ample hole, loosen the soil with spade and fork, and place the bud-union about 4 inches below the soil level. This will eventually cause the shrub to create its own roots in order to replace the stock it is usually grafted upon. Provide good drainage and ample water after planting. A generous amount of fertilizer is required in spring and also after bloom is over. Occasional pruning, including removal of old wood, will keep the plant healthy and abundant.

Dayflower

[COMMELINA COELESTIS]

THIS SPECIES OF *Commelina* comes originally from Mexico and likes a great deal of warmth. Outside of tropical latitudes, where it both self-seeds and roots from its jointed stems, it is strictly a greenhouse plant. The common name of dayflower comes from its short-lived blossoms, which do not shrivel and dry, as is the case with most flowers, but roll up and liquefy into a kind of jelly that bees cannot resist. That liquefying process has led at times to the plant's being called widow's tears.

A certain amount of nourishment is present in the tuberous roots from which *C. coelestis* springs, and both they and the roots of the South American *C. tuberosa* form an agreeable food when boiled and served with the proper white sauce. Another sort, *C. africana,* is used as a purgative, while the most common species in Europe and temperate North America, *C. communis,* provides not only nutrition from its tubers, but also blue pigment from its flowers. Further versatility is shown in *C. nudiflora,* from Asia and North America; its styptic properties aid in the treatment of cuts.

In southern latitudes the dayflower grows outdoors after the tubers are set in the soil. It usually needs greenhouse culture in the north, but may be grown outdoors if the tubers are lifted from the soil before winter, stored until spring, and then replanted. It prefers moist, shady places, but will accept almost any kind of soil; and it spreads rapidly once established. A close relative, tradescantia or spiderwort, may be substituted for dayflower if desired.

Turk's Cap Lily

[LILIUM SUPERBUM]

THIS MAGNIFICENT WILDFLOWER is a native of eastern Canada and the United States, frequenting boglands and meadows from New Brunswick to Ontario and south as far as Arkansas and Georgia. Its recurved petals give it the look of an oriental turban—hence the name Turk's cap, which was borrowed from similar species native to Europe and Asia.

As many as forty blossoms may be found on the stalk of this lily. Its pyramidal form and bright coloration so impressed Peter Collinson, a London nurseryman, when he saw it in bloom that he decided then and there to specialize in North American plants. As it so happened, he was in a good position to do so, for he was in constant touch with John Bartram of Philadelphia (who first sent him this *Lilium superbum*) and with Mark Catesby, who produced the first survey of the flora of North America in 1732. Both contributed many American plants to the gardens of England and Europe.

Turk's cap lilies can grow from five to eight feet high. They are best started from bulbs, since seeds may take from two to four years to flower. In the garden they like some shade over their roots, perhaps a low ground cover of sage, thyme, or bluebells. Lilies resent being crowded and should be set well apart from each other, as they will later form clumps that will need to be divided time and again. A rich soil, lots of moisture, full sun, and a feeding of fertilizer high in potash twice each spring will help them. Soil should be kept moist as long as the plant is in flower and then be allowed to dry for a while. Plant the bulbs early in September, setting them about 7 inches deep. Half an inch of sand surrounding the bulb will discourage plant pests and fungi and aid the drainage of moisture.

Evening Primrose

[OENOTHERA BIENNIS]

EARLY IN THE SEVENTEENTH CENTURY, this plant was sent from its native Virginia to Europe, and quickly became popular in gardens there as the primrose tree. Evening primrose is nocturnal, in contrast to most flowering plants; its blossoms only begin to open at twilight, unfolding so fast that the eye can observe the motion. Its Greek generic name *Oenothera*, or "wine catch," refers to the old belief that its roots caught and held the odor of wine, while *biennis* means "two years." The flower is, of course, not Greek but North American in origin, and is no more a primrose than it is a tulip or a dandelion. Its leaves may be eaten as a salad and its roots are also edible when cooked.

Herbalists have long believed evening primrose to be capable of relieving asthma and whooping cough, and its curative powers have recently been extended to include experimental treatment of multiple sclerosis. Apparently *O. biennis* supplies a form of linolenic acid that is not produced in the bodies of MS victims, but much research remains to be done before it can be called an effective remedy.

O. biennis grows three to five feet high and is powerfully fragrant. Being biennial, it will not flower until its second year, when it will bloom from July to September. It is of very easy culture and may be grown in any ordinary garden soil when planted in either spring or fall. Once established it has a tendency to be self-seeding. For best results, space plants about 12 inches apart. No special care is needed beyond occasional watering.

Japanese Iris

[IRIS KAEMPFERI]

THE SPECIES NAME OF THIS IRIS honors one of the earliest botanical explorers to penetrate the Orient, a German physician named Englbrecht Kaempfer. Between 1683 and 1693, his travels took him from Germany to Sweden and then to Asia, by way of Russia, Georgia, and Persia, along the coasts of Arabia and India, and down to Java, winding up in Japan in 1690—an epic journey in days long before the tourist industry had smoothed the path.

In Japan Kaempfer was chiefly confined to the island of Deshima, to the southwest of Tokyo, and most of his observation and collection of botanical materials had to be done in secret. He may have seen the iris that now bears his name, but he certainly would have had no chance to examine it, for the Japanese were very suspicious of foreigners at that time. Despite everything that hampered his research, Kaempfer was still able to describe many plants never before seen by Europeans in his *Amoenitatum exoticarum,* published in 1712 in his native town of Lemgo, Westphalia. It became one of the sensational successes of his time.

Iris kaempferi, a latecomer to the Occident, is a tall, beardless iris with very large, rather flat, and widely spreading petals. It is best viewed from above, so the Japanese plant it near the foot of sloping banks or build elevated walkways above it. The rhizomes should be planted in a soil enriched with humus that is placed above a moist subsoil. The edges of ponds or streams are ideal. Be sure that no lime is present, for the plants will not tolerate it. They bloom late in the iris season, in June and July.

Virginia Cowslip

[MERTENSIA VIRGINICA]

IN SIXTEENTH-CENTURY AMERICA, this plant was confused with the genus *Pulmonaria,* and the translation of that name, lungwort, became attached to it. Perhaps the early settlers thought they had found a North American relative of that familiar medicinal plant, so useful in treating catarrh and other chest complaints. The Virginia cowslip, however, was found to belong to an entirely different genus, *Mertensia,* and proved a complete therapeutic disappointment since it had no curative properties whatever. Nonetheless it was a beautiful plant, which grew wild in low-lying meadowlands, alongside streams, and in woods rich in layers of humus.

Luckily, Virginia cowslip has adapted well to garden conditions, making a good plant for shaded areas—particularly those that are a bit moist as well. It grows up to two feet in height, and may be found from eastern Minnesota and southern Ontario over to New York, and southward in that corridor as far as Alabama. It is a perennial with a blooming period from March to May, after which it dies down for the season. While it is possible, with some difficulty, to transplant *M. virginica* from the wild, it is much easier and more certain to start it from seed. If seed is gathered from the wild, though, it should be done in late spring and planted outdoors immediately. If seed is purchased, plant it in spring in rich, moist soil, where there is shade. *M. virginica* may also be set into the open border, but in that case try to procure some partial shade for it.

Everlasting Pea

[LATHYRUS LATIFOLIUS]

THE EVERLASTING PEA is a perennial and an old-time garden favorite of European origin. This species can climb nine feet or more by means of its tendrils, which cling to any support offered them. The clinging mechanism is not completely understood, but appears to be the result of pressure within the cells. The tendril, which is actually a modification of the stem itself, projects outward until it blindly touches something. Pressure instantly increases in the cells at the area of contact, causing them to shorten, while the cells on the opposite side begin to lengthen. This sets up a spiral twining, the result of unequal rates of growth, until soon the tendril coils about its support as effectively as a monkey's tail around a branch.

About 160 species of *Lathyrus* are to be found in the north temperate zone, and there are new and improved strains as well. The purplish-rose flowers have a slight fragrance and will bloom abundantly throughout the summer. In fact, the plant may find conditions so much to its liking that it will need control. *Lathyrus* makes a good screen for porches and is readily managed there. Because it retains its color in shady sites, it was once widely used in arbors, although these are rarely found today because of high construction and maintenance costs.

To propagate, plant seeds in the spring in any reasonably good garden soil. For an abundance of blossoms, pick off as many of the young pods as can be reached, letting only a few develop for future seed.

Blue Geranium

[GERANIUM PRATENSE]

THE LONGER FLOWERS are known to man, the more names they tend to accumulate. This is certainly true in the case of *Geranium pratense*, as one can see in this list of its common names: meadow crane's bill, crowfoot, gratia Dei, Odin's grace, bassinets, and even loving Andrew. Opinions about its medicinal value were as numerous among the early herbalists as its names, ranging from none (Dioscorides, first century A.D.) to doubtful (Turner, sixteenth century) to useful, as a styptic for wounds or an astringent against diarrhea (Parkinson, seventeenth century). Parkinson's theories were later confirmed by twentieth-century chemical analysis.

The geranium's name comes from the Greek *geranion*, meaning crane, and refers to the beaklike projections from its fruits. *Pratense* simply stands for "field" or "meadow" in Latin. The plant originated in the Eurasian region and gradually spread westward by way of horticulture, eventually finding its way to America in the course of its travels.

C. pratense is an undemanding plant, which accounts for its increased popularity. The sturdy perennial grows from about sixteen inches to a little over two feet; it makes a welcome addition to the blue garden or to the open border, where it will flower from about the end of April to early June (but only in its second year). Plant seed after frost is over in any good garden soil where it will get sun. To increase the planting divide the clumps in either spring or fall after the plant matures.

Lilac

[SYRINGA VULGARIS]

THE COMMON LILAC, once called blue pipe, is a member of the olive family, and originated in southern Europe, possibly Greece. Though it is chiefly grown as an ornamental shrub, its flowers have been used to flavor syrups and to treat fever. Its fruits were pressed to extract oil of ben, which was used in perfume-making and as an emetic, a purgative (substituting for aloes), an emollient for the skin, and—mixed with warm goose-grease—to relieve earaches.

Lilac has been in European gardens since the time of Henry VIII, and was probably grown even earlier in Islamic countries, where pleasing scents were a prime requisite for garden plants. Many of its named hybrids, however, were developed in France, where there seems to have been a national passion for breeding them. As befits a shrub of great hardiness, the lilac is the state flower of New Hampshire, where the climate is seldom kind to plants.

Almost any well-drained garden soil will do for the cultivation of *S. vulgaris*. For good growth, well-rotted cow manure should be set around the shrub to a height of 4 inches. The manure should be thoroughly worked into the soil, and the ground spaded every two to three weeks in summer. Commercial fertilizers will cause an excess of woody growth. To encourage better flowering, remove old blossoms as soon as they fade, and during the winter prune all branches that do not carry vigorous buds. Repeat the procedure during the following season and at intervals thereafter, so long as the shrub produces ample, healthy blooms. Lilac flowers in April and May in temperate and cool climates, but is not suited to very warm regions. When planting, dig a roomy hole for the roots, and surround them with well-forked soil mixed with manure so that the roots won't be burned.

Zinnia

[ZINNIA ELEGANS]

MEXICO, A COUNTRY THAT HAS GREATLY enriched horticulture, is also the home of this species of zinnia. It was grown in Montezuma's royal botanic garden, where all the plants of his kingdom were displayed, long before the Conquistadors arrived. Horticultural skill was well developed among the Aztecs, and their concept of a comprehensive botanical garden was far in advance of anything to be found in sixteenth-century Europe.

Zinnia elegans, the ancestor of today's annual zinnias, was used in many experimental crosses that led to the production of double-flowered and dwarf varieties. Whatever form a plant may take—tall, short, or what have you—horticulturists will always try to make it into something else. Even though this species didn't reach European cultivation until 1796, its great variability was soon put to work, and double flowers, nearly four inches thick and almost a foot in diameter, were being produced by 1865. The Aztecs would no longer have recognized their old, familiar flower.

Since *Z. elegans* is about three feet high and has blossoms over four inches wide, it is best to use it at the back of the border. Plant seed outdoors in early May, in soil that is deeply dug and well manured. Make shallow furrows with a ruler's edge and plant 3 to 4 seeds per foot. As seedlings develop thin them to 1 per foot. Give them lots of water in hot, dry weather, and put a mulch around them to hold the moisture and keep the soil from packing. Zinnia blooms well in hot weather, and makes an excellent cutting plant throughout the summer.

Spanish Iris

[IRIS XIPHIUM]

EVEN AS EARLY AS 1629, some thirty varieties of this iris were already being grown in England, where it had been introduced from Iberia and North Africa. It naturalized so well in the south of England that it came to be taken for a native species; but John Parkinson, the famous Jacobean apothecary and gardener, correctly stated in his *Paradisi in Sole* that the plant had been brought there by travelers returning from abroad.

Iris xiphium differs from most irises in that it stores future energy supplies in a bulblike organ called a corm, rather than in the usual rootlike rhizome. Spanish iris is a parent of the hybrid Dutch iris, that early springtime favorite of the flower shops. Many horticultural benefits have been obtained from crossbreeding and plant introduction, but caution and wisdom should be exercised when using these techniques, for insect pests, rusts, and blights spread easily into new territories where no natural defenses against them may yet exist. Hybrids may also tend to take over from the native flowers, as they have done in Hawaii, whose natural flora has gradually been replaced by non-native species.

Spanish iris blooms in May in temperate climates; it should not be grown in very cold places. Plant in October in any ordinary garden soil, placing the corms about 6 inches apart and 3 to 4 inches deep. Put them in a sunny, well-drained spot and avoid overwatering. Do not use lime in the soil; rather, some low-nitrogen fertilizer or rotted manure may be worked in well below the corms. Protect plants in winter with a mulch.

Bee-balm or Oswego Tea

[MONARDA DIDYMA]

THE MAN FOR WHOM THIS GENUS WAS NAMED, Nicolas Monardes, was a sixteenth-century Spanish physician from Seville. He described and praised the medicinal virtues of many American plants without ever setting foot in the New World, as specimens were sent back to him in Spain. That explains the term *Monarda; didyma,* however, is a purely botanical appellation, referring to the plant's twin stamens. Its common names came about because bees flock to the scent of this plant and because the colonists in Oswego, New York, used its leaves to make a refreshing tea. It was also traditionally used in treating fever, and contains large amounts of the antiseptic thymol.

Bee-balm reached England in 1744, where its stout growth and bright red color soon made it a universal favorite. The leaves may be used to flavor white wines such as Rhine or Moselle, and they possess a delightful fragrance, much like that of the perfumer's bergamot orange.

Monarda didyma is perennial and blooms from July to September. It is very easy to grow, but does best in a moist, slightly sandy soil. If possible, put it where it will get morning sun, and shade or partial shade in the afternoon; such a procedure will keep it in full flower longer. Oswego tea may be propagated by dividing its clumps in the springtime. Fall division is risky because frost may kill the plant before it can establish itself.

Narcissus

[NARCISSUS TAZETTA]

FEW, IF ANY, GARDEN FLOWERS can boast of a record as ancient as that of the narcissus. It was one of the plants used by the ancient Egyptians for their funeral wreaths, and received mention by the legendary Greek poet Homer. It was supposedly named for the youth who drowned while trying to embrace his own reflection in the water (the narcissus bends its head downward as he did), but Pliny's *Natural History* (from the first century A.D.) says otherwise. There it is claimed that the name comes from *narce,* signifying torpor, because of the narcotic properties of the plant. The bulb contains lycorine, which numbs the entire nervous system and paralyzes the heart, and is more fatal than the youth's self-infatuation.

Narcissus tazetta is now found almost everywhere, and its varieties have given rise to an industry in the mild climate of the Scilly Isles and Cornwall. Tons of them are shipped from there to London every day in the late winter, while other regions are still caught in the gloom and cold.

This species, which grows and blooms in winter, is suited to mild and subtropical regions. In colder regions only the hybrid varieties (*N. poeticus* × *N. tazetta*) may be grown outdoors. Bulbs may be planted to a depth of 6 to 8 inches and placed 6 inches apart. For spring bloom, plant them in October, setting them on a layer of sand. No manure or peat moss should touch the bulbs. Simply give them some commercial fertilizer and humus. Every four years, they should be lifted and divided after the leaves have died back. Dry them in a cool, dry, shaded place and replant in autumn; the bulbs should come apart readily. They need about a month of growth before frost in order to develop roots after replanting. Indoor culture requires a shallow bowl, pebbles, and water. Keep in a cool, shady place and do not expose to excessive light or warmth until roots are well developed. Place them out of the reach of children and pets.

Blue or Great Lobelia

[LOBELIA SIPHILITICA]

WHEN THE INDIANS FIRST informed the white man that this plant was a cure for syphilis, almost every European doctor rushed to put some in his garden. But for once the Indians were wrong, and the European patients had to continue enduring the ravages of a "social disease" that was far too sociable for their liking. Since the plant has emetic properties and causes profuse sweating, perhaps the Indians weren't being altogether guileless and generous with their knowledge, particularly in view of the fact that *Lobelia siphilitica* happens to be poisonous. It is also a little ironic that the flower stands for "social affection" in the Victorian Language of the Flowers. That era may well have been an age of innocence after all!

The blue lobelia is a hardy perennial that grows to about three feet in height and flowers late in the season, extending the period of garden bloom well into autumn. The attractive blossoms are a rich blue, sometimes with a purplish tinge; very occasionally they may be white. The genus is named for a famous sixteenth-century Flemish botanist, Matthias de L'Obel.

Seeds may be planted in the open border as soon as frost is over, or started indoors in February, with the seedlings being moved outside to the garden later. The blue lobelia likes a fairly dry soil, but the red lobelia, *L. cardinalis,* prefers it to be moist. Red lobelia also blooms earlier, from July to September.

Yellow Rose and Rose of India

[ROSA LUTEA and ROSA INDICA]

THE BEAUTIFUL YELLOW ROSE PROBABLY originated in Persia, for much of its early history is bound up with the development of the Islamic garden. It is known that the Muslim rulers of medieval Spain received the flower as a gift from a caliph in western Asia. *Rosa indica,* despite its name, comes not from India but rather from China. Its misnaming was an error made by Carolus Linnaeus, the father of scientific classification, who was a genius in devising ways to bring order out of chaos, but an innocent in accepting data from foreign sources. *R. indica* is an ancestor of the tea rose, and has contributed its trait of perpetual bloom to many hybrids.

Two-year-old field-grown roses are best for planting. Dig a hole that will hold the fully spread root system without any crowding, and line the bottom with a layer of gravel about 2 inches deep. Place rotted manure above the gravel and then cover with a layer of soil. Set the bush in place after cutting away all damaged canes and roots, spreading roots fully and slanting them downward. Add a few inches of loose soil, then gently fill hole with water. When it has drained away fill with earth, lightly tamped and mounded slightly above soil level. Sprinkle a handful of 5–10–5 fertilizer around the plant and add a layer of mulch. Fertilizing should be done on a continuous basis: one handful per average bush in spring, after blooming (or early in July with perpetuals), and finally in early September. A pruning program, removing dead wood and excess canes, will help shape the plant and keep it healthy and abundant. Water rose bushes deeply and frequently for best results.

Monkshood

[ACONITUM NAPELLUS]

THE COWL-SHAPED FLOWERS OF THIS PLANT are responsible for its common name of monkshood. Another name for it is wolfbane, and since bane is an old Anglo-Saxon word for murder, something sinister may be suspected. Despite its beauty, this is a very poisonous plant, related to the not-so-innocent buttercups—many varieties of which have caustic and poisonous properties never hinted at by Gilbert and Sullivan.

One physician to royalty, Pier Andrea Mattioli, actually experimented with monkshood on convicted killers around 1555, in an attempt to see which species were most effective. In Antwerp, at about the same time, some fifty banqueters died when a careless chef accidentally served it in a salad. Monkshood is harmless to the touch, however, and since few people are in the habit of munching on garden flowers, it may be grown without fear; but gardeners who have pets or young children should avoid it altogether.

A. napellus is a showy plant with deep blue flowers, almost indispensable for the blue garden. White and pale blue varieties of this species also exist; other species of *Aconitum* come in lilac, purple, cream, and yellow. Monkshood is perennial; it takes two to three years to bloom from seed, which is the only really practical way to propagate it, since the plant dislikes being transplanted. Some species, however, will permit their roots to be divided. Monkshood grows about four feet high, blooms in late summer and autumn, and will not tolerate tropical or subtropical warmth. About eighty species are known, all of which prefer a rich soil, temperate climate, partial shade, and nearly neutral acid ground.

Wallflower

[CHEIRANTHUS CHEIRI Variety]

CHEIRANTHUS CHEIRI, or wallflower, was also formerly called *Viola lutea,* thus causing some early herbalists to confuse it with those true violas which we call pansies. Often carried at springtime festivals because of its fragrance, it gained the name of handflower, which becomes *Cheiranthus cheiri* in Latin.

The more common name of wallflower comes from a Scottish legend about a border chieftain who was loved by a lord's daughter. Betrothed to a prince, she was locked away from her chieftain in a tower. The chieftain, disguised as a minstrel, sang at the foot of the tower, suggesting that the girl should form a rope ladder to escape. She dropped a wallflower to signal that she understood his message; but either she was poor at tying knots or she used weak materials, for the ladder broke and she plunged fatally to the ground beside the wallflower. The chieftain adopted that blossom as his emblem as he wandered across Europe, singing of his lost love, and the bloom finally entered the Language of the Flowers as a symbol of faithfulness in adversity.

Cheiranthus cheiri likes a warm climate such as that of southern Europe. It blooms very early in the spring and continues into summer. Besides being a border perennial it makes a good rock-wall plant, and will thrive as it does in the wild, with very little attention. The one thing it does dislike is wet winter slush. In colder places treat it as a pot plant, sowing seeds in August and then keeping them in a cold frame until the pots can be set outdoors the following spring.

Forget-me-not

[MYOSOTIS SCORPIOIDES]

FORGET-ME-NOTS COME IN both annual and perennial species. Their flowers, usually blue, can also be white or pink. This perennial species, *Myosotis scorpioides,* gets its botanical name from a far-fetched notion that the leaves resemble the ears of mice, and from the somewhat more accurate resemblance of the curled flower heads to a scorpion's tail.

There is a legend about a medieval knight who, while plucking some of these flowers for his lady on the bank of a swiftly flowing river, fell in and was swept away. Whether or not he was wearing armor at the time the tale does not say; nor is anything said about his ability to swim, although it would seem that he couldn't. All that we are told is that he called out "Forget me not!" as he went downstream—a rather unnecessary remark, since the lady was probably not accustomed to terminating strolls in that fashion. Alas, the story, for all its charm, is not in the least authentic, but pure romantic balderdash instead, dating from about 1803.

M. scorpioides makes an attractive bedding plant around spring-flowering bulbs such as tulip or narcissus. Almost any good garden soil will suit forget-me-nots, but they prefer a situation in partial shade. They like plenty of water and for some reason do better when they are a little crowded—a distinct advantage in a bedding plant.

Carnation

[DIANTHUS CARYOPHYLLUS]

THE SPICY SCENT OF THE CARNATION has led to its being called clove-gilliflower and has contributed greatly to its popularity as a cultivated flower. Recent research indicates that the carnation was probably bred by the Turks about a century before their conquest of Constantinople in 1453. It is a common floral motif on fifteenth-century tiles from Persia and Turkey, but is rarely represented in European paintings of that era. Two exceptions are the *Annunciation of Aix* (1443–44), where it is shown with lily and columbine, and the *Portinari Altarpiece* (1475–76), where it is accompanied by columbine, orange day lily, and iris, which was often confused with lily at that time. In both paintings, the carnation symbolizes the Incarnation of Christ as man—a rather ironic association for a flower developed in the Moslem East. The red color of the flower further signifies the human blood shed by Christ, for red is the color assigned to martyrs.

For cultivation see Christmas Rose and Carnation (page 12).

China Aster

[CALLISTEPHUS CHINENSIS]

IF THIS PLANT WERE LISTED under its proper scientific name, *Callistephus chinensis,* few but botanists and dedicated gardeners would recognize it. The genus *Aster,* limited for the moment to flowers with purple rays, according to one reliable horticulturist, is composed of over three hundred species that hybridize in the wild as prolifically as rabbits breed in a hutch. Even the American botanist Asa Gray, who brought some order among them, admitted, "They reduce me to despair."

Callistephus, although one of the Compositae, an order to which asters also belong, is no more an aster than *Stokesia laevis,* commonly called the Stokes aster. Gray's despair becomes even more understandable when one realizes that Michaelmas daisies are simply asters wearing a misleading common name, which only adds to the confusion.

The China aster is native to China and Japan, and is a highly variable annual that blooms in the autumn. Seeds of this flower reached Paris in 1728, and rapidly gained such favor there that Horace Walpole reported seeing thousands of pots of them in one fourteen-acre Parisian garden.

These plants may be grown in a rich, well-drained soil where they will receive ample sunlight. Their plots should be regularly cultivated to a depth of about an inch; break up the surface soil to a powdery consistency, thus creating a dust mulch to conserve moisture. The plants will also need frequent watering in dry weather. Seed should not be sown until all danger of frost is past. China asters make excellent cutting plants.

Tickseed

[COREOPSIS TINCTORIA]

ORDINARILY THE TERM *tinctoria,* as part of a plant's botanical name, means that it has been used as a dyestuff. Here, however, is the exception to the rule, for there is no record of *Coreopsis tinctoria* ever providing such a substance. Perhaps the botanist who changed its name from *C. elegans* may have wished to reinforce the impression that the flower's pattern of red and yellow resulted from its being dipped in dye.

Tickseed is now only an ornamental plant, a favorite garden flower appreciated for its looks alone, although the American Indians did make a beverage from it and used it to treat heat exhaustion. Its generic name, *Coreopsis,* means buglike in Greek and refers to the shape of its seeds, which resemble ticks. It is a composite, one of a family of about one thousand genera and some twenty thousand species. Each of its blossoms is comprised of two kinds of flowers: the outer, petallike forms, each one complete in itself, are known as ray flowers; the inner disk is made up of hundreds of separate florets compacted into a mass, increasing the plant's chances of successful pollination.

Coreopsis tinctoria may be sown outdoors, after frost, in any ordinary garden soil. It is an annual that will thrive almost anywhere, and prefers being crowded in its site. Bloom is from July to October, which makes it a good cutting plant for the summer garden—one with the added virtue of flowers that last well after being cut.

Lord Chatham's Tulip

[TULIPA Variety LORD CHATHAM]

A BIT OF ENGLISH HISTORY IS REFLECTED in this tulip, which was named after William Pitt, the Great Commoner, shortly after he was made Lord Chatham. Pitt's enormous popularity eventually forced George III of England to include him in the ministry of the kingdom late in 1766. By that time, the king was anxious to find a way of kicking Pitt upstairs and so remove a major obstacle from the path of his campaign to restore full authority to the Crown. Pitt was offered the title of Earl of Chatham, and upon his acceptance he automatically entered the House of Lords, thus losing his political power base in the House of Commons. Pitt's public following reacted immediately to his knighting as a betrayal, and the wily king had little more to fear from him. Nonetheless, if George had allowed himself to be guided by Pitt's moderate policies, he might not have had to contend with the American Revolution.

Lord Chatham's tulip is of the broken variety, whose prized markings cannot be bred because they result from a viral infection that is not genetically transmitted. This particular aberration probably occurred some time in 1767, between the time Pitt's title was conferred on him (after the end of the 1766 tulip season) and the first publication of the tulip's picture in 1768. Three categories of "broken" tulips existed at that time: "rose," a white ground striped with red to scarlet lines; "bybloemen," consisting of purple streaks on a white ground; and "bizarre," with red or brown markings on yellow. Appropriately, Lord Chatham's was a "bizarre," echoing the odd turn of his political fate.

For cultivation see Gesner's Tulip (page 44).

Downy Thorn Apple

[D A T U R A   F A S T U O S A]

THE FLOWERS OF THE GENUS *Datura* are often called angels' trumpets because of their flaring corollas, set atop tubular calyxes. They are relatives of the tomato, eggplant, deadly nightshade, the common potato, and of course the notorious jimsonweed, *Datura stramonium,* which contains poisonous alkaloids that can bring on delirium and death.

Datura fastuosa is a small shrub that seems to have first entered cultivation as a medicinal plant, and only later came to be appreciated for its undeniably attractive flowers. The leaves, mixed with cubebs, sage, and belladonna, were smoked in order to relieve the spasms of asthma. A safer formula combined equal amounts of the ground leaves, certain aromatic substances, and potassium nitrate. Shaped into a cone and burned on a dish, the mixture acted like a fireworks display, producing clouds of herb-scented smoke that promptly relieved the attack. Overuse, however, was found to lessen the effect, as the drug does nothing for the underlying cause. In India, where the plant is indigenous, it is used as a narcotic, a poison, and for the relief of rheumatism and other chronically painful afflictions.

Outdoor culture of downy thorn apple requires a fairly warm climate in spring and summer. It often naturalizes in rich, rank soil in waste places, but does best in sandy loam with leaf mold added. Plant seeds in May, placing them 3 feet apart in shallow furrows and sifting soil lightly over them. Keep soil moist, but don't wash out seed. In dry, hot summers give the plants a mulch of rotted cow manure. Larger plants transplant easily, and once established *D. fastuosa* will thrive in almost any temperate climate. Remember its harmful aspects, though, and look but don't taste!

Chinese Peony

[PAEONIA ALBIFLORA]

THE CHINESE PEONY WAS TWICE introduced into Europe, first by the German naturalist Peter Simon Pallas, who made several extensive botanical explorations into the Siberia and Russia of Catherine the Great. In 1805, after Pallas's specimen had somehow been lost, Sir Joseph Banks of England's Royal Society rediscovered the species. To the vast surprise of all concerned, this white-flowered peony proved capable of producing both pink and lavender descendants. This rather embarrassed the botanists, who had already named it *P. lactiflora,* or milk-flowered peony, but nature is in the habit of overruling botanists from time to time.

In its native China, the peony was called *shao yao,* or herbal spoon flower—none too poetic a name for a blossom that inspired not only beautiful poetry and paintings but also motifs for ceramics and textiles. Cultivated as early as the eighth century in China and Japan, it later spread to Korea, Mongolia, and Siberia. Over one hundred varieties were known in the Orient before the flower was ever brought to Europe. In the T'ang dynasty the peony was considered the King of Flowers and it later became the symbol of the rich and happy man, perhaps because its brightly colored, abundant petals exude a sense of well-being.

Paeonia albiflora should be planted in the fall in a sunny spot on well-drained ground. Prepare the soil beforehand by digging and by enriching with well-rotted manure to a depth of 2 feet. Set the buds on its tubers about 2 inches below the level of the soil and keep fertilizer from direct contact with the roots. Give the plants plenty of water, and feed a handful of bone meal every spring and fall. Avoid heavy mulching at any time. The plant will bloom about June. Cut the growth to the ground in the fall, and do not transplant after the plant has established itself.

Fringed Iris

[IRIS JAPONICA]

THE IRIS HAS A LONG HISTORY OF association with man, and is documented as a garden plant as far back as the fifteenth century B.C., when Thutmosis III brought it back to his palace in Egypt from a conquest in Syria, and had its image carved on the temple walls at Luxor. In medieval times the iris became entangled in some of the legendary history of France in the form of the fleur-de-lis, the sign of royalty. The original model for the emblem, however, had nothing to do with either the iris or the lily. It goes back instead to ancient Babylon and Sumer, where depictions of the sacred Tree of Life, a date palm with protective horns bound to its trunk, gradually evolved into a highly schematic and conventionalized symbol. The cords that held the horns fast to the tree's trunk may still be seen on the fleur-de-lis pattern, but you will look for them in vain on any iris or lily in the garden.

Iris japonica, once called *I. fimbriata,* is an evergreen native to the Himalayas, and blooms in January or February. It may be grown only in greenhouse conditions outside of places where winters remain free of frost, such as Florida and California. The rhizomes should be planted about March in good, ordinary garden soil well lightened with humus, either indoors or outdoors. Set them fairly near the surface of the soil, tamp the soil around each rhizome, and water once or twice a week.

Peony

[PAEONIA OFFICINALIS]

THE LATIN WORD *officinalis,* meaning ''of the shops,'' i.e. apothecary shops, always indicates that a plant had medicinal use at one time or another. The tuberous roots of the peony were believed to cure insanity when hung about a lunatic's neck or simply suspended above him. The antispasmodic effect of tonic steeped from its roots is probably the basis for the belief that it calmed the frenzies of the insane. The perennial was named for Paeon, a legendary physician who used it to cure those gods who were wounded in the Trojan war. It continued to be used medicinally from Homeric times down to the seventeenth century. The peony also had other supposed virtues, such as protecting shepherds and their flocks, warding off storms, demons, and nightmares, and preserving the harvest from damage—a great deal to ask of any plant.

This species of peony appears to have originated in the Mediterranean region. It comes into bloom about May, bearing bright red petals that caused it to signify ''blushing shame'' in the Victorian Language of the Flowers. The plant is now as popular in the modern garden as it once was in the ancient pharmacy. Some double varieties of the species exist.

Paeonia officinalis should be planted outdoors in autumn, in ground that has been readied for it some days before. Choose a well-drained spot, open to the sun and with free circulation of air. Set the plant so that the eyes are about 2 inches below the level of the soil, and keep it well watered at all times. A handful of bone meal given in spring and fall will be most helpful. Use well-aged manure only, keeping it away from the stems and roots. At the end of each season, in autumn, cut the stalks down to the ground and throw them onto the compost heap. Peonies may also be started from seed; sow them in the fall in well-dug beds. A few will germinate by spring, but most will not sprout until the following year. Blossoms will take another year or two to appear.

Blue Windflower

[ANEMONE BLANDA Variety ATROCAERULEA]

THIS TUBEROUS ANEMONE COMES from Greece and Asia Minor, and once bore a botanical name even longer than its present one. John Parkinson, the old English apothecary of Jacobean and Carolean times, called it *Anemone tenuifolia flore pleno purpureo-caeruleo*, which simply means the blue-purple, full-flowered (double) anemone with thin leaves. So many anemones of different colors grow in Asia Minor, especially in Israel, that it has been suggested that they are the Biblical lilies-of-the-field.

Even the seventeenth century had its troubles with pollution, for Parkinson advised against planting windflowers where they may be "annoyed with the smoake of Brewers, Dyers, or Maultkils, which if it be, then will they never thrive well." He also spoke of planting the tuberous roots in August to make them bloom in February, March, and April, adding that some may also be planted in those late winter and early spring months to extend the flowering season.

Anemone blanda cuttings should be planted in seed flats during September, in rich, loamy soil. Winter them in a cold frame at about 40° F., even down to 35° F. briefly, and set them out in early spring in well-drained soil. Give them a spot where they will have partial shade at midday. They may also be grown from seed, sown thinly in cold frames and transferred in early spring to their semishaded, permanent homes in the garden. Keep them cool and don't try to advance their flowering by increasing the heat, or you will lose the crop.

Peruvian Lily

[ALSTROMERIA AURANTIACA]

DESPITE THE PERU IN ITS NAME, this plant comes from a bit further south, being native to Chile. The tuberous roots of this and other species (particularly *Alstromeria ligtu*), which contain a high percentage of starch, are sold as food in Chilean marketplaces. When Carolus Linnaeus received a specimen of *A. pelegrina* from South America, he was so anxious to preserve it from the harsh Swedish winter that he kept it in his own bedroom. He also named the genus for the man who had sent it to him, his friend and pupil, Claes Alstromer.

A. aurantiaca, which means the orange alstromeria, is a tender plant outside of its own habitat—one of those plants that dedicated gardeners love, and the rest of us swear at. Some notion of its determined perversity is evident in its leaves. Each of them twists once as it grows out from the stem, with the result that what should properly be its underside then faces upwards.

The Peruvian lily requires shade, rich soil, and a site that is relatively moist. Its roots increase rapidly, and liquid manure should be given occasionally to keep it healthy. The plant blooms through the summer; as soon as cool, autumn weather begins, lift the plant and store the roots in a dry, cool, but frostfree area for the winter. Set them out again in the spring. To keep a stock for planting, divide the roots at the time of storage, since they seldom will give more than two seasons of bloom each.

Fritillary

[FRITILLARIA MELEAGRIS]

SOMETIMES CALLED TOAD LILY, because of its flowers spotted with maroon
and green, or checkered lily, after its patterned petals, the fritillary always
excites comment and incredulity among those unfamiliar with the plant. It
is said to have been found near Orléans in 1572 by an apothecary and
brought to England shortly after by Huguenots fleeing from France after
the St. Bartholomew's Day massacre. They must have been dedicated
gardeners to have given such care to a plant while running for their lives.

The cup-shaped flower is responsible for its generic name,
Fritillaria—from *fritillus,* a dice cup. *Meleagris* refers to the guinea hen,
whose speckled plumage resembles the spotting of the petals. Luckily for
him, the apothecary who first found it did not experiment with it as a
medicine, for its bulb is poisonous.

Easily grown in the border, fritillary blooms in April or May, and is
perennial, though the bulbs should be divided (and quickly reset) every
third year. Soil should not be rich; well-drained sandy loam mixed with
some small gravel and humus will suit the bulbs. Choose a sunny spot
where some light midday shade is available. Offsets are best for propagation; they should be set about 2½ inches deep into the soil. If rabbits are
around, the fritillaries will need protection, since they are favorite items
on the rabbit menu.

Red-hot Poker

[K N I P H O F I A   U V A R I A]

THIS PLANT, ALONG WITH ALL OTHERS of its genus, was first known as *Tritoma*, a name by which many gardeners still refer to it. Someone, however, decided that the genus should be renamed for Dr. Johann Hieronymus Kniphof, an eighteenth-century professor of medicine and botany at the Academy of Erfurt, Germany. His major contribution to botany was not the discovery of this plant—Kniphof never set foot in Africa, its native habitat—but rather his twelve-volume work *Botanica in Originali*. In it Kniphof reproduced the images of twelve hundred separate plants by applying ink to each specimen and then using it to print its own image. The process took over seven years to complete, and kept Kniphof poor from 1733 well into the 1740s.

Kniphofia uvaria comes from the Cape of Good Hope and entered European cultivation in 1707. The specific name of the red-hot poker, *uvaria*, means clustered, which is a good descriptive term for its flowers. It is a perennial and will bloom from July to September.

Place the plants, which have full, fleshy roots, in sandy, well-drained soil where they will get full exposure to the sun. They need winter protection in regions where the temperature ordinarily goes below 60° F. For the winter months place them under a heavy layer of nonmatting mulch, such as salt hay, so as to avoid rotting. They can also be lifted and stored for the winter in soil boxes in the cellar. They have been favorite bedding plants for many years, flaming as brightly in the garden as their common name implies.

Auricula

[PRIMULA AURICULA]

SWISS MOUNTAINEERS HAVE LONG VALUED the roots of this plant in avoiding vertigo when scaling high places. It also has a reputation for relieving headache, convulsions, and hysteria; perhaps its several chemical constituents do indeed benefit the nervous system. In any case, they keep the flower from being "just another pretty face."

Because they are among the earliest plants to bloom in the spring, auriculas were called *primus* (meaning first), which became *Primula*; *auricula,* or ear, refers to the shaggy outline of the leaf tops, often likened to the ears of a bear. The auriculas now grown are primarily hybrids of *P. auricula* and *P. hirsuta*, but numerous other strains, especially from the Orient, have led to many remarkable variations of pattern and color in this group. They were great favorites of the working classes in nineteenth-century England, but were only rarely grown by the gentry. Now, of course, they are socially acceptable on all levels.

These plants are perennials, blooming in April and May, and may be grown either in borders or in the rock garden. Seeds may be sown in early spring in a soil consisting of 1 part loam, 1 part humus, and ¼ part sand. Plant the seeds about ⅛ inch deep by making an impression with a ruler and later sprinkling soil back over the seeds. They should be watered often, as primulas like a moist (though not soggy-wet) soil, and they will need some shade from the summer sun. Add humus to the plantings from time to time.

Honesty

[LUNARIA ANNUA]

THE COMMON NAMES OF THIS PLANT are many: satin or white satin flower, penny or money flower, silver plate, St. Peter's pence, shillings, money-in-both-pockets, tuppence-in-a-purse, and honesty. All, even the last, refer to its rounded, silvery, and somewhat filmy coin-shaped seed pods. According to the famed American botanist Asa Gray, the name honesty stems from the transparency of the pods, which makes their contents entirely visible. The flower is sometimes called moonwort, though only rarely, because of a possible confusion with a kind of fern commonly known by that name. However, *Lunaria* is Latin for "of the moon," so there is some justification for such usage.

The herbalist John Gerard wrote in 1597 about a Swiss surgeon who mixed honesty with oil, wax, and sanicle leaves (allheal) to make an unguent for wounds. Gerard also recommended it for epilepsy, though without offering evidence of its efficacy. Honesty's four-petaled flowers clearly place it in the *Cruciferae,* or cross-flower, family, all of whose members were considered beneficial according to the old adage "health is in the cross." The plant is allied to mustard, and its mildly biting roots were once used in salads much as we now use radishes.

Whether honesty is annual, biennial, or perennial is still a matter of debate. Perhaps its location or genetic heritage determines what it will do. It rarely blossoms in the first year, but most frequently in the second instead; seldom does it survive for a third year. The fragrant, pink-purple flowers bloom in May and June.

Cultivation is simple; merely plant the pods in any ordinary garden soil and treat them as biennials. The pods are also excellent for dried flower arrangements.

French Marigold

[TAGETES PATULA]

ALTHOUGH THIS GENUS NEVER MADE ANY attempt to conceal its Mexican origins, latter-day gardeners and seedsmen certainly did. They labeled this species French and another one African, though both places were only way stations in the plant's travels after it reached Spain in the very early 1500s. The name *Tagetes* comes from Tages, a grandson of Jupiter, who sprang from a ploughed field in Tarquinia, and revealed the secrets of divination to the Etruscans. But one secret that he did not pass along is the reason why his name was commemorated in this plant, which was not discovered until some two thousand years after his birth.

Although its petals of maroon and yellow are beautiful, French marigold has leaves with an unpleasant odor, one that quickly gave it a reputation for being poisonous to both man and beast. And poisonous it is—but only to a host of pests that wreak havoc underground in gardens. For that reason alone it makes an excellent living pesticide in the kitchen garden, and may be left uncut to bloom in borders outdoors, where nobody's nose will be offended by it.

Sow seeds thinly in March, and pluck out seedlings to a distance of 1 foot. Any ordinary, well-drained garden soil in a sunny spot will do for French marigold. It is an annual plant that blooms in summer, although recent varieties bloom right into frost. Some varieties have been cleared of their musky odor; should some get on your hands, however, rub them with a salt paste, and then wash them in salt water.

Balm

[MELITTIS MELISSOPHYLLUM]

THE BALM, A MEMBER OF THE very extensive mint family, was all but un-known as a garden flower before the sixteenth century. The balm mentioned in earlier literature came from trees that exuded gummy resins, whereas the mint-derived balms all came from the juices of herbaceous (soft-stemmed) plants. *Mel* or *mellis,* Latin words for honey, indicates the attraction of honeybees to this mint and the related *Melissa officinalis*.

Melittis grew wild in many parts of Europe, and decoctions of its leaves were used by herbalists to purify the blood, for healing wounds, as a mild sedative and a diuretic, and in the treatment of diarrhea. *Melissa,* as a tea, was used to ease headaches and toothaches, while the leaves provided a flavoring and were important in the manufacture of a lemon-scented oil used in perfumes and ointments. *Melissa* is planted more often and is known as the common garden balm.

Melissa does well in sun and *Melittis* in semishade, near shrubbery or in borders that receive light shade. Any ordinary, not very rich soil will do, for manure or fertilizer will cause the plants to become leggy in their growth. Turn the soil to a depth of about 18 inches, and work it well with the pitchfork to a fine, crumbly consistency. Be sure the site is well drained, but keep it constantly damp (not wet) by occasional watering and dust-mulching. Seed should be planted thinly and tamped down lightly with a board. Take care not to pack the loosened soil. Seedlings must be weeded and should be thinned if they grow too thickly together. Both *Melissa* and *Melittis* are summer-blooming perennials.

Crown Imperial

[FRITILLARIA IMPERIALIS]

OF PERSIAN ORIGIN, this flower first reached Europe in 1576, where it bloomed in the gardens of the Austrian emperor and thus earned its common name of crown imperial. Carolus Clusius, the famous French botanist of the Renaissance who introduced the plant into Vienna, named it the Persian lily; that name, however, was later transferred to another species, *Fritillaria persicum*.

Its striking appearance soon made the flower well known, and shortly after the London gardens received it (by way of Constantinople), it was mentioned in Gerard's *Herbal*. It even turns up in Act IV of Shakespeare's *Winter's Tale*, where Perdita cites it in a list of blossoms.

The corms of crown imperial give off the smell of a fox's den when rubbed. Despite that strong and disagreeable odor, the Persians ate them—but only after boiling, for they are poisonous when raw.

The strong, stout stem of crown imperial, which can grow three feet high, makes it suitable for the back of a border. Plant it in fall, in deep loam in a well-drained spot, and give it a top dressing of manure just before it begins to flower. It blooms in April or May, and is a perennial bulb that will continue for years. It is best, however, to divide the plants about every three years, placing the offsets back in the soil almost immediately after dividing them.

Meadow Sage

[SALVIA PRATENSIS]

NO OTHER PLANT EXCEEDED the reputation of sage in ancient and medieval times. The Romans once asked, "Why should a man die whilst sage grows in his garden?"; and somewhat later, the English put the saying into verse: "He that would live for aye/ Must eat sage in May." Even its generic name refers to its preservative properties, since the term comes from the Latin verb *salvere,* to save. Some have thought rue should be planted together with it so as to drive away toads, who were reputed to be fond of sage; others believed that the plant withered or shrank according to the fortunes of its owner.

Sage is native to the northern part of the Mediterranean and is supposedly grown at its best in the northwestern regions of Yugoslavia. Despite the presence of many valuable medicinal agents in its leaves, sage is seldom used today for anything other than seasoning. Perhaps the Chinese, who formerly traded three pounds of their choice teas to seventeenth-century Dutch merchants for one pound of sage, knew more about the respective value of plants than they were given credit for.

Salvia pratensis is a hardy perennial that may grow three feet high. Seeds may be started in cold frames in April and the plants moved outdoors when they are large enough to handle and all frost is past. Place them in good garden soil in a sunny position, open on all sides. Give them lots of water in dry weather. Sage is a very variable plant, with different colors and different needs; it has biennial species as well as perennial ones. Honeybees are fond of sage nectar, so beekeepers often grow the plant.

Butterfly Weed

[ASCLEPIAS TUBEROSA]

THIS BRIGHTLY COLORED MEMBER OF THE milkweed family differs from the others in that its stalk secretes little or none of the thick, milky fluid that gives the group its common name. The derivation of its botanical name is simple: *Asclepias* for the Greek god of medicine, and *tuberosa* for the tubers on its roots. These roots were once boiled and used for food by the American Indians, and decoctions of the roots were used as an expectorant to relieve the pain and congestion of pleurisy. The plant was formerly listed in the *United States Pharmacopeia* and also in the Department of Agriculture's publication *American Medicinal Plants of Commercial Importance*. Since then it has been determined to be dangerously toxic, and preparations containing the plant are being banned.

Butterfly weed is a native North American plant, and may be found from Maine to southern Ontario, and south as far as Arizona, Texas, and Florida. It is one of the showiest of wild flowers, and has been brought into the garden for just that reason. The plant grows about two feet high and blossoms from July to August or later. True to its name, it does attract butterflies whenever they are around. You may gather the seed from wild plants in the fall or buy it from seedsmen. Plant it in the spring in dry, sandy soil, where it will get plenty of sun and heat. Field-grown plants may also be purchased from some nurseries.

Foxglove

[DIGITALIS PURPUREA]

IN EARLIER TIMES, FOXGLOVE WAS USED chiefly to cure excessive phlegm or to treat scrofula, but no one thought to use it for heart conditions. No one, that is, until 1875, when the English physician William Withering began to investigate the high degree of success attained by an elderly village woman who relieved cases of dropsy by giving sufferers the leaves of this plant. Dr. Withering published his findings that same year, but it was not until the early nineteenth century that the cardiac properties of foxglove began to be fully realized.

The plant's botanical name, *Digitalis*, is Latin for "the measure of a finger." Its common name is very apt, for one can easily imagine a dapper Reynard drawing the blossoms over his paws. It has also been called witches' thimbles and fox bells. As valuable as it is to medicine, foxglove has a dangerous side as well; excessive amounts of digitalis are poisonous, causing irregular heartbeat and lowering blood pressure. The antidote is another poison with opposite effects, *Aconitum napellus*. Grow it for the eye's pleasure, but tack up a mental sign: "Beware the foxglove!"

Although the plant is perennial, it is better treated as a biennial. Plant seed in early spring in any ordinary garden soil. Foxglove likes a cool, damp climate such as may be found in coastal areas, but since it once grew wild, it is sturdy enough to adapt to any reasonable garden conditions. It will bloom in early summer and may grow four feet high, or even twice that height in favorable locations.

Pansy

[VIOLA TRICOLOR]

THIS OLD-TIME FAVORITE, which was bred in English gardens from its wild form, has been called by several names over the centuries, a sure sign of a long association with man. It has been known as herb trinity (from the three colors), love-in-idleness, pansy, three-faces-in-a-hood, cull-me-to-you (hold me to you), and heart's-ease, to cite but a few of the two hundred and more names given to it in England and continental Europe.

Apparently the pansy had a reputation for comforting more than the heart, for the Elizabethan herbalist Gerard said that it "doth wonderfully ease the paines of the French disease." That may also explain the name love-in-idleness, especially in view of the legend that the flower had been wounded by one of Cupid's arrows. In Elizabethan times, the plant was used medicinally for agues, convulsions, epilepsy, lung and chest ailments, external sores, ulcers, and itching. Several active constituents are indeed present in the pansy, and it was once recognized as official in the *United States Pharmacopeia*.

For cultivation see Pansy Varieties (page 14).

Pelargonium Hybrids

[PELARGONIUM DAVEYANUM Varieties]

IN NATURE THERE ARE ABOUT 230 SPECIES of pelargoniums, tremendously diverse in appearance. Some seem like succulents; others have a trailing habit of growth, and still others seem well on their way towards becoming woody plants, although all are herbaceous. Like so many other members of the plant world, they are constant reminders that evolution is an ongoing process.

The beak-shaped fruits, which bear some resemblance to a stork's beak, are responsible for the botanical name of this genus, which is based on the Greek word *pelargos,* meaning stork. The closely related geraniums, often confused with the pelargoniums, get their name from the Greek word for crane, *geranos*; and still a third related genus, *Erodium*, is derived from *erodios*, or heron. It is almost as if Audubon had temporarily turned botanist. Immensely popular as house plants and garden flowers, pelargoniums are nonetheless no longer as frequently hybridized as they were in the nineteenth century. At that time they were still novelties from the Cape provinces of South Africa, and were generally sold as geraniums.

Pelargoniums are plants for the cool greenhouse (night temperatures of 45°–50° F.), though they may be planted outdoors in places that never fall below those levels. Start seed in a flat of compost mixed with sand, and keep it at about 55° F. until the young plants can be transferred to 5- to 6-inch pots, filled with a mixture of earthy loam, coarse sand, and some rotted manure. A teaspoon of bone meal may be mixed in as well. Some liquid manure will aid flowering. Keep plants a bit on the dry side in winter. In early spring increase watering gradually, while also giving them some slight warmth. Full sun and good ventilation are needed, especially after flowering.

Hollyhock

[ALCEA ROSEA]

THE GARDEN HOLLYHOCK SEEMS ALWAYS to have been part of traditional and country gardens, but it actually wasn't introduced from China until 1573. Other species of mallows, especially *Alcea officinalis* (marshmallow), are native to Europe and were known and used much earlier. Most of the colonists who came to America brought seeds of one kind or another with them to ornament their simple homes and gardens. Spires of bright pink or white hollyhock enlivened many an otherwise bare spot. It was easy to grow, a virtue in communities that had little time for any concern beyond mere survival. Its popularity naturally led to a number of common names, one of which was hockleaf, since that plant was used to cure swollen heels in horses. An erroneous notion that the plant came from the Holy Land, combined with the name hockleaf, soon transformed the term into ''holy-'' or ''hollyhock.'' Another popular name, cheeses, comes from the shape of its seed pods, so like the wheels of cheese with which every farmer was once familiar.

Hollyhocks will grow almost anywhere and often spring up spontaneously. Any good garden soil will do for them. A bright, sunny place, where the lowermost leaves are free from shade, is best. Since the plants grow five or more feet high, they should be set at the back of a border, somewhat apart rather than massed for the best effect. Care should be taken to keep the roots covered with soil. They are better treated as biennials than perennials, and should be started in flats outdoors at the height of summer. Thin out the seedlings before frost and cover with a straw mulch during winter. In the spring plant them in their permanent home, roots pointing directly downward, at a little greater depth than when in the seedbed.

Dutch Iris

[IRIS XIPHIUM Variety]

THE DUTCH IRIS, THAT EARLY SPRING favorite of the florists' shops, is a hybrid iris that results from a cross between *Iris xiphium* (Spanish iris) and *I. tingitana* (Tangiers iris). The term Dutch is probably due to a family of Dutch nurserymen named Tubergen, who were the first to succeed in breeding a very early blooming iris from the species mentioned above. Oddly enough, while both ancestors came from areas where the soil was somewhat dry, their offspring prefers ground that is moist. Cultivation does change the habits of plants, and many species now found in gardens have little in common with their wild forebears.

For cultivation see English Iris (page 28).

Amaryllis

[AMARYLLIS BELLADONNA]

THE NAME AMARYLLIS OFTEN stirs up visions of a lovely young shepherdess beautifying the meadows of ancient Greece. Actually, she was an unsophisticated country girl whose home, according to her creator, the poet Theocritus, was in rural Sicily. The plants that bear her name also stray a little from the facts sometimes: they may really be *Crinums, Brunsvigias, Sprekelias,* or even *Hippeastrums*; so it is perhaps just as well that gardeners continue to use the term *Amaryllis* for the sake of convenience.

As a matter of fact, this flower was totally unknown in either ancient Greece or Sicily, since it was first introduced into Europe from the Cape of Good Hope, South Africa early in the eighteenth century. Its appeal was instantaneous and the amaryllis soon became one of the most popular of plants, for it could be grown indoors in cooler climates or outdoors in warmer ones.

As a house plant amaryllis must be given a long rest period, from late fall to early spring. Bulbs should be lifted after the plant has bloomed and its leaves have fully developed; the bulbs will then have enough food in them for safe storage. During their growing season water regularly and give liquid manure every 2 weeks. A little extra food just before blooming helps. The bulbs may be dried, though not to the point of shriveling, in dry sand, and then stored in a cool, dry place. Repot them in early spring, keeping them at about 65° F., in 1 part gritty sand, 1 part humus, 2 parts loamy soil, ½ part dried cow manure (useful also for making liquid manure), and 1 tablespoon of bone meal, all well mixed.

Propagate new plants in the fall by cutting the old bulbs in halves or quarters, keeping bits of the base and stem attached to each piece. These should be planted in a potting soil made from equal parts of humus, loam, and gritty sand. Place the pieces stem portion upright, from 2 to 2½ inches deep. Keep the pot well watered and at about 60° F. In approximately 3 months, shoots will spring up and new bulbs will form from each piece.

Periwinkle Varieties

[VINCA MINOR Varieties]

ORDINARILY THE PERIWINKLE has blue flowers, but as is often the case, horticulturists couldn't rest until they had developed pink and white varieties such as the strains shown here, and caused the single blossoms to double. These efforts date back as early as the beginning of the eighteenth century, but seemed to have been wasted when some of the varieties later became lost to cultivation. Luckily, the breeders had done a better job than they thought, for some of the "lost" plants turned up again, growing in the wild as escapees from gardens.

No one knows why the common name of periwinkle became attached to both a small shellfish and this flower, since neither resembles the other. However, it is likely that the old Latin *pervinca*, which became *pervenche* in French, was corrupted into "periwinkle" in early medieval times. The flower was also called joy of the ground in the fourteenth century; today one species, *Vinca rosea*, is the joy of physicians, for it harbors some anticancer properties that may aid cancer patients.

Vinca minor is a hardy evergreen that trails across the ground like ivy and makes a good ground cover for shady areas. It is sometimes called creeping or running myrtle, though it has nothing to do with that genus. Plants may be placed in any ordinary garden soil, out of the sun. Be sure to loosen the soil well, but then firm the individual plants in it just enough to keep them anchored. Propagate by cutting young shoots in summertime and then rooting them before transplanting. This may be done in a cold frame in an equal mixture of sand and soil; water often and keep in shade. The frame should be opened about 1 hour per day, and the tips of the growing plants pinched back so as to encourage full, bushy growth.

Hyacinth

[HYACINTHUS ORIENTALIS]

NATIVE TO THE TERRITORY that runs from the Balkans through Greece to Asia Minor, the hyacinth was known to the ancient Greek herbalists only as a wild plant. They used it as a diuretic, in the treatment of dysentery and venomous spider bites, and—somewhat incomprehensibly—to prevent puberty in young boys. Perhaps they wanted to be assured of a good supply of boy sopranos, much like the famous Italian *castrati* of later times.

Hyacinth is thought by some to have first been cultivated in Persia, while others suggest Turkey. One thing is certain, however, and that is that the modern plant does not look like anything mentioned in ancient times, for hyacinthine referred to golden hair. Although hyacinths never caused the furor that surrounded the tulip, some bulbs did sell for as much as two hundred pounds each in the eighteenth century. One anxious fancier even preserved a precious bulb within a birdcage, safe from attack by mice or rats, until it could be propagated. As early as 1730, methods of forcing the bulbs into earlier bloom for greater productivity underwent experimentation at the Chelsea Physic Garden in London.

Hyacinths like partial shade and a sandy soil well enriched with humus. They are heavy feeders and need plenty of water while growing. All cultivated forms come from *Hyacinthus orientalis*. The bulbs should be set from 5 to 6 inches deep to protect them in winter, and a winter mulch in areas that go just below zero should be given as additional insurance. Production and quality will vary naturally from year to year. Propagation is usually done by seed, but offset bulbs may be used if the plant is fed heavily during the first two growing seasons. Set the bulbs 4 inches deep in a sunny place in spring and give 5–10–10 fertilizer; transplant in the fall.

Windflower

[ANEMONE CORONARIA]

THE BIBLICAL LILIES-OF-THE-FIELD have been thought to be any of several flowers, from the Madonna lily, a rarely seen native of Israel, to the tulip, iris, and martagon (Turk's cap) lily. Reams of paper have been used up in building convincing cases for each, but nonetheless *Anemone coronaria* still emerges as the favorite candidate of both botanists and Biblical scholars. The confusion over its identity arose because the Hebrew word for lily is *shusan*, a fairly vague term that can refer to any brightly colored, lily-shaped flower. While bright enough to be a lily, the windflower does not exactly have the requisite shape, and its leaves, with their multiple points, lack anything lilylike about them; so perhaps some other possibility may yet turn out to be the Biblical prototype.

The windflower has been called Venus's tears, after those the goddess shed over the slain Adonis. The plant was also used in wreaths and garlands, as the Latin *coronaria* signifies. In addition, it has served as a curative charm, tied around the arm or worn about the neck. This traditional usage persisted from ancient Egypt down to Victorian Britain, and may still be going on today.

A. coronaria is a tuberous rooted perennial that blooms from February to April. It is best grown as an indoor plant, except in warm climates such as California or Florida. In the fall, place its tubers in roomy boxes of rich soil, slightly lightened with sand. Let them grow at cool temperatures, 40° to 45° F., watering regularly and providing good drainage. When the leaves have ended growth, stop watering altogether, and do not resume until early September, when the next season's cycle may be started up. By no means should any attempt be made to speed up flowering by adding heat, for that may kill the plant.

Snapdragon

[ANTIRRHINUM MAJUS]

THE COMMON SNAPDRAGON is also called toad's-mouth, which it resembles, and lion's-mouth, which it does not. The abrupt way in which the tube of the flower closes over pollinating bumblebees explains its ordinary name of snapdragon well enough, but the botanical one of *Antirrhinum* is another matter. That term is derived from the Greek, and means "resembling a snout," not "against" it as the prefix *anti-* normally implies.

Antirrhinum majus, a perennial native to the Mediterranean region, was once cultivated for the oil extracted from its seed, a substance similar to olive oil. In ancient Greece it was said that the plant brought renown to those who were anointed with it—a cheaper road to fame than hiring a public-relations firm. The plant was also believed to ward off sorcery.

A. majus usually reaches a height of about three feet. Seeds may be started in a cool place indoors in January or February. Sow them in seed flats, and after germination move them to a cold frame, gradually toughening them before setting them into the garden. At the time of planting, outdoor temperatures should be 45° F. at night and about 60° in the day. Place the plants about 10 to 12 inches apart and water well to settle soil around their roots. Keep them dry until vigorous growth begins and then pinch off all but 4 to 6 of the healthiest shoots. As they grow, pinch off any side shoots that may develop. At about 15 inches of growth start light sprinklings of fertilizer until blooming begins. They will produce cut flowers through the summer.

Sunflower

[HELIANTHUS ANNUUS]

ALTHOUGH THE INDIANS KNEW THE FOOD VALUE of this native American plant long before the rest of the world, even they could not have guessed at all of its possibilities. The annual sunflower seed crop now exceeds 7 million tons and yields some 280 million gallons of oil, which has commercial use in the paint, varnish, soap, and pharmaceutical industries, as well as in the manufacture of salad oil, margarine, synthetic lard, and oil cake for fodder. Sunflower leaves and stalks provide silage for winter cattle feed, and the meaty seeds are a favorite snack of both children and birds. In the past, its leaves were used as a tobacco substitute, and the stems, treated like flax, were made into a silky fiber. The Elizabethan herbalist John Gerard tells us that "the buds . . . boiled and eaten . . . after the manner of artichokes . . . surpass the artichoke far in procuring bodily lust." Even if adult hopes may be dashed a bit in that respect, the plant still offers more than one might reasonably expect from any single source.

This annual can grow as high as twelve feet, although seven to eight feet is average; it has a heavy flower head twelve inches wide. It should therefore be given good, firm staking as support. Its blooming season is from July through September, when the seeds should be harvested. Sunflowers may be started from seed outdoors in early spring, after frost has ended. Plant the seeds where they are to grow, about ½ inch deep in rich, moist soil that has been well and deeply worked. Place them about 1 to 2 feet apart in a row that runs east to west, so that the flower heads may turn with the sun. Sunflowers may also be started in seed flats in March, and then set in a cool place until they become strong enough to be transplanted. Professional growers often mound up earth around the stems to a height of about 6 inches to give extra support against wind breakage.

Stonecrop

[ROCHEA COCCINEA]

THIS SOUTH AFRICAN MEMBER of the stonecrop family is a succulent plant. The leaves and stems of such plants store water in their cells as protection against the seasons of drought that they often encounter in their native habitats. To prevent loss of the stored fluid by transpiration and evaporation, stonecrop's stomata (small mouthlike openings on the underside of the leaves) open only in the cool of night, and the plant's surfaces are further protected by a thick, waxy skin. Stonecrop is usually found growing in and over rocks, hence its common name. The plant bears a densely packed bouquet of tubular, fragrant, bright red florets at the terminal of each stem. It is a popular florist's plant with long-lasting bloom and may be grown outdoors in warm, dry places, or as a house plant in temperate regions.

All succulents are somewhat prone to damage by nematodes, so make certain to use sterilized potting soil. A good potting mixture is 2 parts of gritty sand, 2 parts silty loam, 1 part crushed brick, and ½ part humus. Add 1 tablespoon each of bone meal and hydrated lime. Maintain good drainage that carries off all excess moisture, letting none stand about the roots. This is easily done by filling the planting pot to one quarter of its depth with broken clay shards before adding soil. Give stonecrop plenty of sunlight and water in summer, or place it out of doors in pots buried in sand or ash. A good summer temperature for the plant is 65° to 75° F., and it should not be exposed to temperatures below 55° F. in winter. If bright leaf color is desired on indoor specimens they may be brought to near freezing for a few days and given no water. Unhealthy plants develop a pale, anemic color, usually the result of insufficient light or too much water.

Propagate by cuttings, allowing the ends to dry or heal over before putting them in dry sand. Give the cuttings plenty of light and air, but do *not* water.

Plantain Lily

[HOSTA SIEBOLDIANA]

THE PLANTAIN LILY OBTAINED ITS COMMON name through its lily-shaped flowers and plantainlike leaves, which are vaguely similar to those of the roadside weed, the great plantain. It has also been known as funkia, and many still refer to it by that name. However, it has now been placed in the genus *Hosta*, named after the Austrian botanist N. T. Host. All the species of this genus are native to China and Japan, and came to the West about 1790. The first of these flowers to arrive was given yet another name, *Hemerocallis coerulea* or blue day-lily, but that quickly proved to be an error of classification.

The specific term in *Hosta sieboldiana* commemorates yet another physician for the Dutch East India Company, Dr. Philipp Franz von Siebold of Germany. His major botanical achievements were the introduction of many plants from the Orient and his two-volume work *Flora Japonica,* which remains a prime source of information on the plant life of Japan. But somehow, whenever and wherever Siebold went in Japan he stirred up trouble. In 1828, in one of his many brushes with the law, he was caught smuggling maps out of the country. He was lucky enough to get off with a jail sentence; some of his Japanese collaborators were executed.

H. sieboldiana is perennial and blossoms in midsummer. However, its true beauty lies in its large heart-shaped foliage, with its deeply furrowed, symmetrical venation. It likes shade, but will also do well in the sun of the open border or in the rock garden. To preserve the beautiful blue-green color of the leaves, do *not* give it fertilizer. Plantain lily is of the easiest cultivation, simply requiring a moist soil. The clumps may be divided in either spring or fall.

Canterbury Bells

[CAMPANULA MEDIUM]

IN LATIN THE WORD *campanula* means little bell, an apt term for the flowers of this widespread genus of about three hundred species. *Campanula medium* is native to Spain, France, and Italy, which means, of course, that it has to be added to the list of pilgrims who made their way to Canterbury. In fact it has been conjectured by some that the resemblance of these flowers to the small bells used to caparison the pilgrims' horses led to the naming of the plant.

Canterbury bells have also been known as Mercury's violets, viola mariana, mariets, and Coventry bells. This last name caused a controversy that lasted for years among herbalists. One of them, John Gerard, mistakenly said that it grew plentifully in the wild around Coventry—hence the name. But a short while later an apothecary of Coventry, one Brian Ball, claimed that *C. medium* grew there only in gardens. The European herbalists Mattioli and L'Obel took the species to be Canterbury bells, *C. medium* (which it was), but John Parkinson incorrectly thought he saw some differences in the flowers and held to the name Coventry bells, which properly belongs to another campanula, *C. trachelium*. No matter what it was called, the plant was a cultivated one, and grew wild in England only where it had escaped from gardens.

Besides being ornamental, *Campanula medium* is edible; its parsnip-like root may be boiled and eaten with salad oil, vinegar, and pepper. It blooms from May to August, but when raised from seed it will not flower until the second year, as it is a biennial.

For culture see Bluebell-of-Scotland (page 42).

Cornflower

[CENTAUREA CYANUS]

ONCE UPON A TIME the science of botany was in such a dreadful state that one botanist, who should have known better, believed that grain sown in a bad year would come up as cornflowers instead. This would have proven doubly unfortunate for the farmer, as cornflower has a troublesome habit of dulling the edges of cutting implements—hence its alternate common name of hurt-sickle.

Although there are those who consider it to be nothing more than a weed, cornflower has also been prized as a garden bloom since ancient times. The Egyptians planted it beside their garden pools almost four thousand years ago, and it remained in favor as a garden plant even down to Tudor and Jacobean times in England. The ancient Greeks thought that Chiron the centaur taught Achilles about cornflower's usefulness in healing wounds, a belief that led to its generic name of *Centaurea. Cyanus,* the species name, refers to the vivid blue of the flower's blossoms.

Cornflower is an annual of the easiest possible cultivation. Simply sow the seed in springtime in almost any garden soil and the plant will make the most of it. Cornflowers rather enjoy being crowded, which saves the task of thinning. However, they can sprawl quite a bit if left on their own, so they will need trimming from time to time to keep them within limits. There are double varieties of *Centaurea cyanus,* and the summer-blooming plant is sometimes known as bluebottle or ragged sailor.

Japanese Anemone

[ANEMONE JAPONICA]

IN 1844 AN ENGLISH PLANT HUNTER named Robert Fortune found this flower growing abundantly in the area around Shanghai, particularly on grave sites, where it was frequently planted. Until then it had been thought native to Japan, but the truth was that it had only been introduced there. Fortune sent a live plant back to England, and scarcely had it arrived before it was crossed with another anemone from Nepal. This hybrid made its way rapidly into horticultural use, and other hybrid forms were derived from it, with the result that everything about the Japanese anemone, from its origin to its proper identity, became confused. And then, to muddy things up even more, the wild ancestor of *A. japonica,* lost for centuries, was rediscovered in 1908, growing happily in the southern Chinese province of Hupeh. It was named *A. hupehensis* after its place of habitation, and the relationships and names of that plant and its progeny have been a puzzle fit for a Philadelphia lawyer ever since.

A. japonica, a perennial, is a late-blooming flower, making its display from late September until frost. In China it flowers as late as November, but Shanghai stays warmer in the fall than do most areas of the United States and Europe. It will grow in almost any soil and is best grown from root cuttings. Simply chop the root lengths of a plant into pieces 2 inches long, and set them in a seed flat under an inch of soil. As the shoots spring up, pot them in separate small pots and place them in a cold frame for the winter. Plant outdoors in spring.

Avens

[GEUM CHILOENSE]

THIS PLANT WAS INTRODUCED FROM CHILE around 1874, and promptly added to the already rampant confusion in the realm of botanical nomenclature. It was sold as *Geum coccineum*, a rarely cultivated plant from Asia Minor, and its South American ancestry was thus totally denied—entirely without reason. It is one of the very few herbaceous plants of the rose family to have found a place in garden borders, cinquefoil being the only other horticulturally important one.

Other members of this genus, those which were native to Europe, were called avens, and so that common name became attached to this species, too. Almost all avens have sweet-smelling roots, which bear the scents of clove or cinnamon and are sometimes used to flavor gin. One famous species was called herb bennet, i.e. herba benedicta or blessed herb, because of its reputation for driving off demons and evil—a property that could still prove very useful in our own times. The roots of avens were said to dissolve internal blood clots, relieve colic and venomous bites, and act as a carminative or anti-flatulent—an altogether commendable plant.

These flowers are easily grown in any ordinary garden soil. They prefer the cooler sections of the north and south temperate zones. A perennial, *G. chiloense* is the most popular member of its genus for use as a border flower, blooming from late June to September. Plant seed in spring in soil worked to a spade's depth, making sure to set it where it will get full sun. The roots may be divided in late September, while seeds are gathered for spring planting.